Answers to the Top 85 Questions About Jesus

REALFAITH.COM

BY MARK DRISCOLL

Answers to the Top 85 Questions About Jesus
© 2023 by Mark Driscoll

ISBN: 979-8-9877121-2-2 (Paperback)
ISBN: 979-8-9877121-3-9 (E-book)

Unless otherwise indicated, scripture quotations are from The Holy Bible, English Standard Version, copyright 2001 by Crossway Bibles, a publishing ministry of Good News Publishers. Used by permission. All rights reserved.

All emphases in Scripture quotations have been added by the author.

No part of this publication may be reproduced, stored in a retrieval system, or transmitted in any form by any means, electronic, mechanical, photocopy, recording, or otherwise, without the prior permission of the publisher, except as provided for by USA copyright law.

CONTENTS

4 Questions about Jesus' Birth...................1
6 Questions about Jesus' Family....................6
18 Questions about Jesus' Humanity......................13
4 Questions about Jesus' Divinity.......................34
5 Questions about Jesus' Ministry..................... 40
5 Questions about What Jesus Taught.....................46
3 Questions about Jesus' Relationship with the Father........ 52
5 Questions about Jesus' Relationship with the Holy Spirit.....57
4 Questions about Jesus' Battle with the Demonic............64
9 Questions about Jesus' Betrayal and Death...............70
10 Questions about Jesus' Resurrection.....................82
6 Questions about How People Knew Jesus was Coming......94
6 Questions about What Jesus is Doing Right Now..........102

Appendix - The Most Important Question of All:
    Do You Know Jesus?...................109

Additional Resources from Pastor Mark....................112
End Notes.................................... 113
About RealFaith and Pastor Mark........................ 115

4
QUESTIONS ABOUT JESUS' BIRTH

1. How was Jesus conceived?...........................2
2. When was Jesus born?............................... 3
3. Where was Jesus born?..............................4
4. Who was present when Jesus was born?................5

1. How was Jesus conceived?[#]

An angel Gabriel appeared to Jesus' mom, Mary, and told her some amazing but scary news: Your son will be named Jesus, which means, "God saves from sins." Rather than worrying, however, we find her worshipping in Luke 1:46-55. Mary belts out a beautiful, spontaneous, anointed, worshipful song in response to God's goodness and long-awaited provision.

Worship encompasses all of life, but it most assuredly includes singing. Mary sings, "My soul magnifies the Lord." Her son will be God's Son and her Savior. God can take a virgin like Mary and give her a son. "For nothing will be impossible with God".[a]

God can create everything out of nothing. God can take on human flesh and enter into human history as the man Jesus Christ. God can atone for the sin of the world on a chunk of wood. God can rise from death. God can raise us from death. God can hear and answer prayer. God can take enemies and make them friends. Nothing is impossible with God. That's why Christians can be joyful and hopeful even amidst horror. That's why we sing and pray. Our God is a God of the impossible.

---

[a] Luke 1:37

2. When was Jesus born?#

The opening sentences of Luke chapter 2 demonstrate the author's great attention to historical detail. Luke introduces us to Augustus Caesar, who was ruling at the time that Jesus was born.

Augustus Caesar was a very significant political leader who ruled over the Roman Empire, one of the most prominent, longstanding, far-reaching empires in the history of the world. He was the adoptive son of Julius Caesar. His title "Augustus" means "the majestic or highly revered."

Historians say that during his rise to power Augustus Caesar was ruthless, but once he assumed power, he become more benevolent. He was a fairly gracious ruler compared to others in his day, far more so than people like King Herod, who was a maniacal man through the totality of his life. Working under Augustus Caesar was a governor named Quirinius, who enforced and executed policies and decisions from the Emperor.

Luke locates the birth of Jesus in a specific historical timeframe by telling us that it occurred during a census ordered by these rulers. Caesar Augustus reigned over the entire Roman Empire, and Quirinius served as a sort of cabinet member to the senior leader. Caesar would demand a certain action, and a man like Quirinius would execute on the order. In this case, Luke tells us, a census was to be taken, which would have been a means for Caesar to assess his vast power and command maximum tax and military participation from the populace.

3. Where was Jesus born?#

The prophet Micah in the Old Testament provides a clue about Jesus' birthplace hundreds of years in advance. The special child would be born in Bethlehem: "But you, O Bethlehem Ephrathah, who are too little to be among the clans of Judah, from you shall come forth for me one who is to be ruler in Israel, whose coming forth is from of old, from ancient days".[a]

In the original Hebrew, "from ancient days" can mean "from eternity." Despite a long journey and no place to stay but an animal stable, Joseph and Mary arrive in Bethlehem safely, just in time for Jesus to be born. The Creator and King of the Universe's first throne on earth is a feeding trough for animals.

In this humble gesture, however, we see God's sovereign power over governments and history. God arranged the details implemented by everyone from the powerful (Caesar Augustus and Quirinius) to the powerless (Joseph and Mary), not to mention the infinite number of lives and events leading up to that point, in order to fulfill his Word and demonstrate his lordship over all.

[a] Micah 5:2

4. Who was present when Jesus was born?#

People thought shepherds were odd. They lived by themselves, outside of town, sleeping in the open, and surrounded by animals all the time. Their reputation was less than stellar. Shepherds were stereotyped as crooks and thieves, and they couldn't even testify in court. It didn't help that they couldn't leave their flock without risking their livelihood, which means they couldn't make it to the temple for sacrifices and feasts and maintain the same religious devotion as the rest of God's people. In short, the shepherds were not highly regarded in their society.

When an army of angels lit up the sky to announce God's birth into history, no one would have ever expected them to break the news to a bunch of shepherds. Upon hearing the big announcement, however, the shepherds outside of Bethlehem hurry off to find the baby boy. Besides Mary and Joseph, these anonymous outcasts are the first people in the world to enjoy an audience with Jesus Christ. It's curious how God arrives in a humble way to a humble family and announces the event to the humble shepherds. God works with them for His glory, by His grace. Years later, Jesus even described Himself as the Good Shepherd who lays down his life for the sheep.[a] God redeems an unpopular profession, showing that He is humble and willing to look after us like sheep. Contrary to common belief, the wise men didn't visit Jesus until He was about 2 or 3 years old, so they were not present at His birth.

[a] John 10:11

6
QUESTIONS ABOUT JESUS' FAMILY

5. Who was Jesus' mom?.................................7
6. Who was Jesus' earthly dad?......................8
7. Who were Jesus' brothers?........................9
8. Who was Jesus' cousin?............................10
9. What was Jesus' family heritage?.............11
10. Did Jesus' family worship Him as God?...12

5. Who was Jesus' mom?#

As the mother of God, Mary is the most significant woman in the history of the world. Mary was very young at the time—as young as age 12—but she was betrothed to be married to a man named Joseph. A lot has been said about this couple, especially every year at Christmastime. Mary was possibly illiterate, since very few rural young women were formally educated in that day. Her connection to God included singing, praying, and remembering the Scripture she had heard in synagogue. Unlike the matronly depictions common in medieval artwork portraying Mary as a pampered princess, she was actually a peasant girl with a simple well-worn dress and dirty hands and feet from manual chores.

Almost all of the theologians I've read believe Mary was somewhere between 12 and 14 years old. Let that sink in. The fact that the couple was "betrothed" meant that Joseph and Mary had pledged to marry each other, an arrangement far more serious and binding than what we understand as engagement today. Terminating a betrothal required divorce proceedings, though a betrothed couple would not live together or consummate until after marriage. Together with their families, Joseph and Mary would have been anticipating a humble, joyful wedding ceremony.

6. Who was Jesus' earthly dad?#

Small-town religious gossip can be brutal. Joseph married a single mom and adopted her son. Joseph had to deal with the fact that his boy was called illegitimate, his wife was called unfaithful, and he was called a fool for the rest of his life. He didn't have to accept this fate. Joseph would have been well within his rights to abandon Mary—technically, he could have even sought to have her stoned to death for adultery. But God told Joseph to love Mary and raise the child, and that's exactly what Joseph did. Thanks to Joseph's humble obedience, Jesus had a dad. And Matthew 1-2 provides more details about him.

For you single men reading this, do not overlook the single mothers God places in front of you as a possible wife for your consideration. It is almost certain that when Joseph sat in his youth group with his friends and compiled a list of qualities he was looking for in a wife, the virgin Joseph did not include "pregnant" on his ideal list. Yet, there is no more godly and glorious woman, wife, and mother the world has ever known than Mary.

7. Who were Jesus' brothers?&

Have you ever wondered what it would have been like to share a bunk bed with Jesus as a kid? Mark 6:2 tells us, "Is not this the carpenter, the son of Mary and brother of James and Joses and Judas and Simon? And are not his sisters here with us?" Jesus had at least 4 brothers and 2 sisters, but no one is sure of the exact number.

One of Jesus' brothers, James, wrote a book of the Bible bearing his name. During his ministry, James earned the nickname "James the Just." It also appears that James was a man of action who refused to tolerate a church that consumed the good news of Jesus but did not respond with good deeds like Jesus. As the leader of a large, powerful church, James saw a bunch of Christians who said they loved his big brother but did not act like Him at all. He was very serious about the reputation of his Big Brother, which explains his passion and pointedness.

In Jude 1, Jesus' other brother introduces himself as, "Jude, a servant of Jesus Christ and brother of James."

In Galatians 2:9, Paul calls James a pillar holding up the church along with Cephas (Peter) and John.

Both James and Jude go on to be devoted Christian pastors, worshipping their big brother Jesus and writing books of the Bible bearing their names.

8. Who was Jesus' cousin?[#]

If we took a nationwide poll to name the greatest person history has ever known, it's highly unlikely that John the Baptizer would even crack the top ten or top thousand. But the Bible is clear that John is preeminent. First of all, we read in Luke 1:15, that John "will be great before the Lord." Jesus makes it even clearer a few chapters later saying, "I tell you, among those born of women none is greater than John".[a] This is an incredible statement, especially when you consider the fact that John spent the majority of his life living in obscurity. He began his public ministry in his late twenties or early thirties, and although he drew a lot of attention, it only lasted a few months before Jesus showed up. John was thrown in prison shortly thereafter, where he was beheaded as a young man. What was so great about this bug-eating, honey-chugging, gospel-preaching, sinner-baptizing eccentric? From Zechariah's prophesy and elsewhere in the gospels, we can glean at least seven aspects of John's greatness and true greatness in the sight of God.

1. John came from Spirit-filled parents
2. John was filled with the Holy Spirit
3. John humbly prepared the way for Jesus
4. John was an evangelist
5. John made the invisible kingdom visible
6. John obeyed God's call on his life
7. John avoided adolescence

[a] Luke 7:28

9. What was Jesus' family heritage?#

Joseph was of the family line of David, and David grew up around Bethlehem. For the census, everyone returned to the original hometown of their family. In order to obey the law, Joseph took pregnant Mary on a roughly hundred-mile journey from Nazareth to Bethlehem. It's a terrifying prospect, when you think about it, with the very real possibility she could give birth to God on the side of the road far away from any doctor, medical care, or help whatsoever. But God, in His providential sovereignty, orchestrated history to get this couple from Nazareth to Bethlehem in order to fulfill the prophecy of Micah 5:2 about the Savior's birthplace. Despite a long journey and no place to stay but an animal stable, Joseph and Mary arrive in Bethlehem safely, just in time for Jesus to be born. The Creator and King of the Universe's first throne on earth is a feeding trough for animals. In this humble gesture, however, we see God's sovereign power over governments and history. God arranged the details implemented by everyone from the powerful (Caesar Augustus and Quirinius) to the powerless (Joseph and Mary), not to mention the infinite number of lives and events leading up to that point, in order to fulfill His Word and demonstrate His lordship over all.

10. Did Jesus' family worship Him as God?[@]

The Bible tells us that when Jesus first started preaching, His family "went out to seize him, for they were saying, 'He is out of his mind'".[a] James, Jesus' half-brother, was originally opposed to the claims of deity by his brother[b], but a transformation occurred in James after he saw his brother resurrected from death.[c] James went on to pastor the church in Jerusalem and authored the New Testament book bearing his name. Jesus' mother Mary was part of the early church that prayed to and worshiped her son as the Son of God, along with James and Jude.[d] Jesus' brother Jude also wrote a book of the New Testament bearing his name. It is impossible to conceive of Jesus convincing His own mother and brothers to suffer persecution in this life and choose the torments of Hell in eternal life for worshiping Him as the one true God unless He proved His deity by resurrecting from death.

[a] Mark 3:21 [b] John 7:5 [c] 1 Corinthians 15:7 [d] Acts 1:14

18
QUESTIONS ABOUT JESUS' HUMANITY

11. What did Jesus look like. 14
12. What is incarnation?. 15
13. Did Jesus experience the normal parts of life?. 16
14. Did Jesus experience the painful parts of life? 17
15. Did Jesus have a sense of humor?. 18
16. What was Jesus like as a child?. 20
17. What was Jesus like as a teenager?. 21
18. What did Jesus do for work?. 22
19. Was Jesus fully man?. 23
20. Did Jesus make mistakes?. 24
21. Did Jesus face temptation?. 25
22. What was Jesus' prayer life like?. 26
23. How did Jesus maintain a healthy emotional life?. 27
24. How did Jesus pick friends?. 28
25. Did Jesus suffer?. 30
26. Why Did Jesus come to earth?. 31
27. What was Jesus' personality?. 32
28. Did Jesus read the Bible?. 33

11. What did Jesus look like?[1]

Despite no biblical or historical evidence, many attempts have been made to depict the appearance of Jesus Christ. The truth is that He was a young healthy carpenter who worked with His hands and walked a lot. He was from the town of Nazareth, but many people mistake that with the Old Testament Nazirite vow of Samson to not get a haircut or drink alcohol[a], when the New Testament says that long hair on a man was gender confusion.[b]

The Byzantines put a beard on Jesus as a symbol of power. The Victorians made Jesus blond. Out of the more than fifty mainstream films made about Jesus, He has never been played by an actor who is ethnically Jewish. Recently, "Popular Mechanics" had a search for the face of Jesus. Essentially every film about Jesus done prior to the days of the radical 1960s emphasized the deity of Jesus. Seven of the first ten reel movies ever made were about Jesus and had the word "passion" in the title. The first feature-length movie of Jesus was made in 1912 and titled "From the Manger to the Cross", or "Jesus of Nazareth". The legendary director and devout Christian Cecil B. DeMille literally transformed movie special effects with his 1923 film "The Ten Commandments". In 1927, he also produced the life of Jesus in the movie "King of Kings". In that film he was very careful to portray Jesus as very pious with little humanity; he even had a glowing aura around him, which made Him appear like something of an icon on the screen.

[a] Numbers 6 [b] 1 Corinthians 11:14

12. What is incarnation?[%]

Incarnation (from the Latin meaning "becoming flesh") is the word theologians use to explain how the second member of the Trinity entered into human history in flesh as the God-man Jesus Christ. One prominent theological journal explains:

The English word "incarnation" is based on the Latin Vulgate, "Et ver- bum caro factum est." The noun caro is from the root carn- ("flesh"). The Incarnation means that the eternal Son of God became "flesh," that is, He assumed an additional nature, namely, a human nature.[1]

The incarnation is expressly stated in John 1:14, "And the Word became flesh and dwelt among us, and we have seen his glory, glory as of the only Son from the Father, full of grace and truth."

13. Did Jesus experience the normal parts of life?

When we think of Jesus, sometimes we think of Him as Clark Kent and Super Man, as if He sometimes was human and sometimes was immune from human problems. That's not the case. Jesus was both fully human and fully God at all times, so many aspects of His life were staggeringly normal, including:

- Being born of a woman
- Having a normal body of flesh and bones
- Growing up as a boy
- Having a family with brothers and sisters
- Obeying His parents
- Worshiping God and praying
- Working as a carpenter
- Paying taxes
- Getting hungry and thirsty
- Asking for information
- Having male and female friends He loved
- Giving encouraging compliments
- Loving children
- Celebrating holidays
- Going to parties
- Loving His mom

14. Did Jesus experience the painful parts of life?[1]

Although He was God, Jesus was not without pain while He took on human form. Here are just a few examples of how Jesus experienced pain, though there are many more in the Gospels:

- Financial problems – poor, stolen from
- Satanic problems – attacked, tempted
- PR problems – slander including of His mom
- Legal problems – arrested, convicted
- Relational problems – denied, abandoned, betrayed
- Emotional problems – "man of sorrows" in Isaiah, no wife or kids to enjoy or comfort Him
- Physical problems – weary, nap, hungry, thirsty, needy crowds, beaten, killed

The book of Hebrews tells us that Jesus went through hard stuff so that He could empathize with us in our suffering and weakness, because as we know, there are some things you learn in school, and others you learn in the school of suffering.

15. Did Jesus have a sense of humor?[1]

Joy appears over 200 times in the Bible, laugh/laughter appears over 40 times. Elton Trueblood wrote an entire book entitled "The Humor of Christ", which studies 30 Gospel Passages. Here are some of my favorite passages:

> "there are numerous passages . . . which are practically incomprehensible when regarded as sober prose, but which are luminous once we become liberated from the gratuitous assumption that Christ never joked...Once we realize that Christ was not always engaged in pious talk, we have made an enormous step on the road to understanding."

> "Christ laughed, and...He expected others to laugh...A misguided piety has made us fear that acceptance of His obvious wit and humor would somehow be mildly blasphemous or sacrilegious. Religion, we think, is serious business, and serious business is incompatible with banter."

Additionally, the "Dictionary of Biblical Imagery" says, "If there is a single person within the pages of the Bible that we can consider to be a humorist, it is without a doubt Jesus...Jesus was a master of wordplay, irony, and satire, often with an element of humor intermixed".

Here are some examples of Jesus' humor to study for yourself:
- Plank & speck[a]
- Camel & needle[b]
- Peter – Rocky & Satan[c]
- Jesus made fun of religious praying[d], fasting[e], tithing[f], leadership[g], silly rules[h], so that they were offended by Him[i], and said we would be blessed if we took Him seriously but not ourselves so we would not be offended.[k]

[a] Matthew 7:3 [b] Matthew 19:24 [c] Matthew 16:13-20 [d] Matthew 6:6 [e] Matthew 6:16 [f] Matthew 23:23 [g] Matthew 15:14 [h] Matthew 15:10-14 [i] Matthew 15:12 [k] Matthew 11:16

16. What was Jesus like as a child?#

It may not seem like much information, but Luke 2:40 provides some indication of Jesus as a boy: "And the child grew and became strong, filled with wisdom. And the favor of God was upon him." Luke 2:52 adds, "Jesus increased in wisdom and in stature and in favor with God and man." The Lord Jesus grew physically from boyhood through adolescence to manhood. He grew spiritually, studying the Scriptures, worshipping, and praying. He grew socially in favor; people respected him enough to call him a rabbi, even in his hometown. It would seem that Jesus likely did not receive a formal education as a traditional rabbi, as a teacher. But in Nazareth there would have been a synagogue where perhaps dozens of people at a time would get together for prayers and readings. These were very simple, rural folk, many were likely illiterate. Jesus was literate, so He received some education somehow. All evidence suggests that Mary and Joseph did do a great job raising Jesus. They taught Him, they loved Him, they served Him, they protected Him, and they got Him a great education.

17. What was Jesus like as a teenager?#

The Bible tells us very little about Jesus' early years. Luke gives us our only glimpse of what He was like as a teenager. Luke 2:41-52 tells the story of the boy Jesus, visiting the temple with His family. Though He was only 12 years old, Jesus was discussing theology with grown scholars who were amazed at His knowledge. He was very theologically astute and a very devoted student of Scripture. Not only that, but as we shall see He was also a boy of great courage and character. In this same episode, Jesus' parents lose track of Him. Mary was absolutely terrified. Jerusalem had a population of around 100,000, and they're used to Nazareth, a village of maybe around 100. Somewhere among the crowds, the caravans, and the conversations of the big city, Joseph and Mary realize they've lost God. Literally. That's an especially bad day, but every parent can identify with that same horrible feeling of having a young child wander off. Jesus' mother and father began searching desperately, "in great distress".[a] They had brought Jesus to Jerusalem as a young man, perhaps gave Him some freedom to roam, and then proceeded to lose Him. They finally track Him down in the temple, and His response is fascinating. "Why were you looking for me?" He asks, "Did you not know that I must be in my Father's house?"[b] The religious establishment treated the temple with unhealthy adoration. For Jesus, it was simply His dad's home. He wasn't there to look good or act religious. He just liked to hang out with God His Father.

[a] Luke 2:48 [b] Luke 2:49

18. What did Jesus do for work?#

Jesus didn't grow up in a large house; He grew up in a small house. He didn't have access to the best education; He was in a small town with many illiterate people. Jesus didn't grow up wearing the finest clothes; He dressed simply. His earthly father wasn't a king; His daddy was a carpenter, and He helped His dad put food on the table for His family. He likely worked in carpentry until the public launch of His ministry at age 30.

19. Was Jesus fully man?[%]

The Bible affirms the humanity of Jesus Christ in a variety of ways. Jesus had a human name—Jesus (meaning "Yahweh saves") Christ (meaning "anointed one")—and a human genealogy.^a He was born of a woman^b, had brothers and sisters^c and was racially Jewish.^d Jesus grew physically, spiritually, mentally, and socially^e, learned^f, experienced fatigue^g, slept^h, grew hungryⁱ, and thirsty^k, worked as a craftsman^m, had male and female friends He lovedⁿ, gave encouraging compliments^o, loved children^p, celebrated holidays^q, went to parties^r, loved his mom^s, prayed^t, worshiped^u, and obeyed God the Father.^v

Furthermore, not only did Jesus have a physical body^w, but He also suffered and died "in the flesh".^x In addition to His body, Jesus also had a human spirit.^y Jesus was emotional as well, for the Bible notes that Jesus experienced grief^z, had compassion^{aa}, was stressed, was astonished^{cc}, was happy^{dd}, told jokes^{ee}, and even wept.^{ff}

^a Matt. 1:1–17; Luke 3:23–38 ^b Matt. 1:18–25; Luke 2:7; Gal. 4:4 ^c Matt. 13:55 ^d John 4:9 ^e Luke 2:42, 52; 3:23 ^f Matt. 4:12; Mark 11:13–14; Luke 2:40, 52 ^g Matt. 8:24; Mark 4:38; Luke 8:23–24; John 4:7 ^h Mark 4:36–41 ⁱ Matt. 4:2; Mark 11:12; Luke 4:2 ^k John 4:7; 19:18 ^m Mark 6:3 ⁿ John 11:3–5 ^o Mark 12:41–44 ^p Matt. 19:13–15 ^q Luke 2:41 ^r Matt. 11:19 ^s John 19:26–27 ^t Matt. 14:23; Mark 1:35; 14:32–42; John 17 ^u Luke 4:16 ^v John 5:30; 6:38; 8:28–29, 54; 10:17–18 ^w Rom. 8:3; Phil. 2:7–8; Heb. 2:14; 1 John 4:2–3 ^x Rom. 8:3; Eph. 2:15–16; Col. 1:21–22; Heb. 2:14; 10:19–20; 1 Pet. 2:24 ^y John 12:27; 13:21; 19:30 ^z Matt. 23:37; Luke 19:41 ^{aa} Matt. 9:36; Mark 1:41; Luke 7:13 ^{bb} John 13:21 ^{cc} Mark 6:6; Luke 7:9 ^{dd} Luke 10:21–24; John 15:11; 17:13; Heb. 12:2, 22 ^{ee} Matt. 7:6; 23:24; Mark 4:21 ^{ff} John 11:34-35; John 8:40; Acts 17:31; 1 Tim. 2:5

20. Did Jesus make mistakes?[+]

Some think that sin and mistakes are synonymous, when they are in fact different things. A sin is a moral wrong, and a mistake is a morally neutral imperfection. Those who do not understand this distinction painfully try to live lives of perfectionism and are devastated at mistakes that do not trouble God and therefore should not trouble them. Parents that fail to recognize this distinction discipline their children not only for sins but also for mistakes. Do you think that Jesus accidentally knocked over a glass of water as a kid, or forgot to do His chores, or made a mess? He sure did. While He did not sin, He did make mistakes, because He was human.

21. Did Jesus face temptation?[+]

Prior to His death on the cross Jesus' greatest spiritual battle was with the devil himself. Knowing Jesus was isolated, hungry, thirsty, and tired after forty days alone fasting in the wilderness, Satan sought to exploit Jesus' humanity. Satan offered the hungry Jesus bread to eat. Satan also offered self-indulgence to meet every physical longing that we humans have, such as food, drink, sex, sleep, and comfort. The Father offered self-denial to resist every sinful longing and temptation that we face. Often we think of the ministry of the Holy Spirit as being miraculous things, but the Holy Spirit also ministers in the mundane. He is there to help you in times of trouble, trial, and temptation so you can live by a supernatural power, the most incredible power source there could possibly be!

22. What was Jesus' prayer life like?[+]

In Luke 11:1, the disciples say to Jesus, "Lord teach us to pray," and Jesus responds in Luke 11:13, "If you then, who are evil, know how to give good gifts to your children, how much more will the heavenly Father give the Holy Spirit to those who ask him!" Jesus' answer to the request "Teach us to pray" is about receiving the gift of the Holy Spirit, because, while Trinitarian prayer is directed to the Father, it is empowered by the Holy Spirit. The Holy Spirit actually teaches us how to pray and Jesus Himself prayed by the Spirit in Luke 10:21-22. This prayer of Jesus is described as "rejoicing in the Holy Spirit," indicating that the Son's prayer to the Father is conducted in the joyful power of the Holy Spirit. This is a beautiful description of worshipful prayer that shows us how the Spirit empowers us to pray. In Mark 14:36, Jesus prays "Abba, Father, all things are possible for you. Remove this cup from me. Yet not what I will, but what you will." This prayer shows us both Jesus' relational intimacy with God (calling him "Abba," which means something akin to "Daddy") and His submission to the Father's authority and will. In this example we learn two things: prayer to the Father should always be respectful but need not be formal. Throughout the Gospels, Jesus prayed Scriptural prayers, long prayers, warfare prayers, thankful prayers, prayers in song, and desperate prayers with His last breath. He prayed often, fervently, honestly, and sincerely.

23. How did Jesus maintain a healthy emotional life?=

Jesus had a lot of enemies, including those who maligned His reputation, religious neat nicks who were more conservative than God and always wanted to pick a fight, a constant parade of people draining His energy, and a group of people that literally wanted Him dead. There is surprisingly very little written about the emotional life of Jesus in comparison to such things as His teachings, miracles, and parables. Theologians have struggled with the emotions of God in general, and Jesus in particular. Let's consider Jesus' emotional life. For the first time as a man, Jesus dealt with physical exhaustion, the adrenaline rush that can compel us to a fight or flight response, and the kind of dishonor, disrespect, and disregard from people that can quickly push a person toward being emotionally unwell. Add to that the fact that Jesus did not have a loving wife and fun kids to come home to, and the pressures He faced would crush anyone else. Nonetheless, Jesus maintained a perfect emotional life in a world filled with circumstances that were far from perfect. Part of the Holy Spirit's ministry in the life of Jesus was directing His emotions. As one example, Jesus' joy came from the Holy Spirit according to Luke 10:21, which reveals, "Jesus, full of joy through the Holy Spirit…" (NIV). Later on, we read the same thing of the emotional life of Jesus' disciples in Acts 13:52, "the disciples were filled with joy and with the Holy Spirit." Because Jesus lived by the Spirit and sent the Spirit to empower our lives, we can live by the same power, growing in the same character and emotional health of Jesus Christ.

24. How did Jesus pick friends?=

Surveying the life of Jesus, it is insightful to see how He managed so many diverse, complex, and shifting relationships with the help of prayerful time with the Father and Spirit. The following are eight laws of relationships observed in the life of Jesus.

1. **The law of hospitality:** Jesus was friendly to all people, but He was friends with only a few people.

2. **The law of capacity:** Relationships are costly. A close relationship costs time, money, and energy. In the Bible, we read of all the people Jesus met with, prayed for, taught, and healed. But there is an even longer list of all the people that Jesus did not meet with, pray over, teach, or heal.

3. **The law of priority:** For Jesus, His inner circle of three disciples plus a few friends and perhaps His family got the majority of His personal time and energy.

4. **The law of seasonality:** Most relationships are seasonal. Few are for life. Jesus grew up with people in a small town, but we don't hear much of anything about those people.

5. **The law of safety:** When it comes to people, we should love all but trust few. Love is free. Trust is earned. Jesus loved everyone but did not trust everyone. People trusted Jesus, but Jesus did not trust all people.

6. **The law of clarity:** A transition talk is an opportunity to lovingly but clearly define (or redefine) the lane the relationship will be. Jesus had this kind of transition talk with Peter. Jesus also had a closure conversation with Judas, who was overtly evil.

7. **The law of idolize-demonize:** In a short amount of time the enthusiastic crowd shouting, "Hosanna, hosanna," soon became the hateful mob crying, "Crucify, crucify." This sick cycle continues in today's celebrity culture where we build people up to tear people down and then build someone else up to repeat the cycle.

8. **The law of economy**: Relationships are like vehicles. Some relationships get good gas mileage. These relationships don't drain our energy and tend to keep moving forward without a lot of drama or difficulty. Other relationships, however, get lousy gas mileage.

25. Did Jesus suffer?

Jesus suffered and yet He was blessed because the Holy Spirit rested upon Him in glory during His suffering. By the time Jesus reaches His final week, He has already been run out of His hometown as a prophet without honor. Jesus ominously begins talking openly about His impending death. Jesus sits down with His Jewish disciples to eat the traditional Passover meal that God's people have been eating ever since their deliverance from bondage and slavery in Egypt as recorded in Exodus. The types of suffering that Jesus endured include spiritual suffering, mental suffering, emotional suffering, financial suffering, relational suffering, public suffering, physical suffering, personal suffering, and total suffering when He died for us on the cross.

26. Why did Jesus come to earth?%

Plain and simple, Jesus came to earth to deal with our sin problem once and for all. In Acts 2, Peter begins by affirming that Jesus fulfills the promises of a divine Messiah, God come among us, with miracles, signs, and wonders, showing that He is both Lord and Messiah (vv. 22, 36). Next, Peter declares that Jesus died on the cross according to God's prophetic purpose (v. 23). Then he proceeds to emphasize the reality that God bodily raised Jesus from death in fulfillment of Old Testament prophecy (vv. 24–32). Peter concludes with the final acts of God exalting Jesus above all the demonic powers to the right hand of the Father and pouring out the Spirit in fulfillment of Old Testament prophecy (vv. 33–35). This revelation is of God's work for us in the life, death, burial, resurrection, and exaltation of Jesus Christ, who poured out the Spirit on His church.

27. What was Jesus' personality?%

Most Christians view Jesus Christ as either Lion or Lamb and not both. Those of us with more lamb personalities will focus on the parts of the Bible where Jesus was meek, kind, patient, loving, and appears more passive if not even timid. Those of us with more lion personalities will focus on the parts of the Bible where Jesus was strong, firm, urgent, controversial, and appears more active, if not aggressive. The Bible presents Jesus as both a Lion and a Lamb. Looking into eternity and the realities of Heaven and Hell, Revelation 5:5-6 says, "Weep no more; behold, the Lion of the tribe of Judah, the Root of David, has conquered, so that he can open the scroll and its seven seals. And between the throne and the four living creatures and among the elders I saw a Lamb standing, as though it had been slain, with seven horns and with seven eyes, which are the seven spirits of God sent out into all the earth." Jesus is both tough as a Lion and tender as a Lamb. In Heaven, King Jesus will rule as a tender Lamb. In Hell, King Jesus will rule as a tough Lion.

28. Did Jesus read the Bible?=

Luke 2:46–47 says that at the age of twelve in the temple in Jerusalem, Jesus was "sitting among the teachers, listening to them and asking them questions." Jesus' knowledge of the Scriptures was so insightful that "all who heard him were amazed at his understanding and his answers." To mature in the ways of God, you have to know the Word of God.

4
QUESTIONS ABOUT JESUS' DIVINITY

29. Did Jesus say He was God?.........................35
30. Did Jesus perform miracles?.......................36
31. Was Jesus fully God?..............................37
32. Are there any extra-Biblical texts that confirm Jesus' divinity?...................................38

29. Did Jesus say He was God?[%]

Jesus refused to be considered merely a good moral instructor and instead claimed to be "God alone".[a] Additionally, those who heard Jesus say these kinds of things wanted to kill Jesus because He was "making himself equal with God".[b] Jesus' claims to be God were clearly heard and understood by His enemies, and Jesus never recanted.[c] John 8:58–59 reports that Jesus said, "'Truly, truly, I say to you, before Abraham was, I am.' So they picked up stones to throw at him, but Jesus hid himself and went out of the temple." In John 10:30–33, Jesus also said: "'I and the Father are one.' The Jews picked up stones again to stone him. Jesus answered them, 'I have shown you many good works from the Father; for which of them are you going to stone me?' The Jews answered him, 'It is not for a good work that we are going to stone you but for blasphemy, because you, being a man, make yourself God.'" In Revelation 22:13, Jesus says, "I am the Alpha and the Omega, the first and the last, the beginning and the end." With these titles, He is obviously referring to Himself as eternal God.

[a] Mark 10:17-18 [b] John 5:18 [c] Mark 14:61–64

30. Did Jesus perform miracles?[%]

The nearly 40 miracles that Jesus performed throughout the New Testament demonstrate God is with Jesus. Just as miracles confirmed the authority and anointing of the ancient prophets and Jesus' apostles, the miracles of the Messiah are God's way of giving His stamp of approval to the claims of Jesus. They point to Him as the person through whom God is doing His work. For example, when Jesus gave sight to the blind man, the people would have been reminded of Psalm 146:8: "The LORD opens the eyes of the blind." The fact of Jesus' miracles is so well established that even his enemies conceded it.[a]

[a] John 3:2; 5:36; 10:25, 32, 37-38; Acts 2:22; 10:38

31. Was Jesus fully God?[%]

Jesus is nearly universally recognized as a great moral example, insightful teacher, defender of the poor and marginalized, humble servant to the needy, and unprecedented champion of overturning injustice with nonviolence. However, the divinity of Jesus Christ is most frequently and heatedly debated. Simply stated, the question as to whether Jesus Christ is fully God is the issue that divides Christianity from all other religions and spiritualities. There are many reasons why we believe Jesus was fully God:

1. God the Father said Jesus was God[a]
2. Demons said Jesus was God[b]
3. Jesus said He was God[c]
4. Jesus is given the names of God (Son of Man, Ancient of Days, Jehovah, Alpha and Omega)
5. Jesus' miracles confirm that He is God[d]
6. People worshiped Jesus as God
7. Jesus repeatedly invited people to pray to Him as God

[a] Hebrews 1:8 [b] Mark 1:34 [c] Matthew 26:63-65 [d] John 10:36-39

32. Are there any extra-Biblical texts that confirm Jesus' divinity?[1]

The resurrection of Jesus Christ is one of the most well-documented events in ancient history. Here are some examples of accounts of the resurrection outside of the Bible:

Josephus was a Jewish historian born just a few years after Jesus died. His most celebrated passage, called the "Testimonium Flavianum," says:

> "Now there was about this time Jesus, a wise man, if it be lawful to call him a man; for he was a doer of wonderful works, a teacher of such men as receive the truth with pleasure. He drew over to him both many of the Jews and many of the Gentiles. He was [the] Christ. And when Pilate... had condemned him to the cross...he appeared to them alive again the third day, as the divine prophets had foretold these and ten thousand other wonderful things concerning him."[2]

Suetonius was a Roman historian and annalist of the Imperial House. In his biography of Nero (Nero ruled AD 54–68), Suetonius mentions the persecution of Christians by indirectly referring to the resurrection:

> "Punishment was inflicted on the Christians, a class of men given to a new and mischievous superstition [the resurrection]".[3]

Pliny the Younger wrote a letter to the emperor Trajan around AD 111 describing early Christian worship gatherings that met early on Sunday mornings in memory of Jesus' resurrection day:

> "I have never been present at an examination of Christians. Consequently, I do not know the nature of the extent of the punishments usually meted out to them, nor the grounds for starting an investigation and how far it should be pressed... They also declared that the sum total of their guilt or error amounted to no more than this: they had met regularly before dawn on a fixed day [Sunday in remembrance of Jesus' resurrection] to chant verses alternately amongst themselves in honor of Christ as if to a god".[4]

5
QUESTIONS ABOUT JESUS' MINISTRY

33. What role did prayer play in Jesus' ministry?........... 41
34. What role did miracles play in Jesus' ministry?......... .42
35. How did angels empower Jesus' ministry?............. 43
36. How did Jesus serve outcasts?...................... .44
37. What did Jesus say that no one else has said?.......... 45

33. What role did prayer play in Jesus' ministry?[+]

Throughout Jesus' ministry, we see Him praying to the Father. Some of His most famous prayers are in the Garden of Gethsemane, the Lord's Prayer, and the High Priestly Prayer in John 17. In the Garden, Jesus is about to head to his crucifixion and pours out His heart to the Father, asking if the cup of suffering can be removed from Him. Ultimately, we see Jesus' remarkable submission to the Father as He accepts His will and goes on to be crucified. Throughout the prayer, He is in anguish and expressing his fears, concerns, and pain to God. In the Lord's Prayer, Jesus gives the disciples a model of how to pray, beginning with remembering that God is Father, thanking God, asking for His provision, confessing sin, forgiving others, and asking for His protection. Lastly, the High Priestly Prayer in John 17 is one of my favorites. Jesus starts by praying for His own relationship with the Father and that He would align with the Father's will. Then He prays for Christians, that they would be guided by the Holy Spirit, and ultimately that non-Christians would meet the Father and become part of His family.

34. What role did miracles play in Jesus' ministry?*%

Roughly twenty-seven times in the Gospels we see Jesus heal an individual. Roughly ten times we see Jesus heal entire groups of people.[a] Jesus performed other verified healings not recorded in the Bible.[b] Specific deliverance miracles Jesus performed through the Holy Spirit include healings from bleeding, epilepsy, deafness, muteness, and blindness.[c] Once Jesus returned to Heaven following His healing from death, some wondered if God would continue to heal people. Doctor Luke wrote his follow-up book, Acts, which reports the supernatural acts of the Holy Spirit through Christians who continued the Spirit-filled ministry of Christ. Just as the Holy Spirit descended upon Christ at His baptism, the Holy Spirit then descended upon Christians so that they could live by His power and continue His kingdom ministry.

[a] Matt. 4:23–25; 8:16; 12:15; 14:14, 34–36; 15:30; 19:2; 21:14; Luke 6:17–19 [b] John 20:30 [c] Luke 13:11–16; Matt. 17:14–18; Mark 7:35; Matt 9:22–23; 12:22

35. How did angels empower Jesus' ministry?*

Angels served in Jesus' earthly life in 13 ways:
1. An angel promised the birth and ministry of John the Baptizer.[a]
2. An angel named Jesus.[b]
3. An angel told Mary she was chosen to be Jesus' virgin mother.[c]
4. An angel told Mary and Joseph to parent Jesus.[d]
5. Angels told the shepherds Jesus was born.[e]
6. Angels worshipped Jesus at His birth.[f]
7. Angels warned Jesus' parents of the coming genocide so they could flee to Egypt.[g]
8. Angels strengthened Jesus after His temptation battle with Satan.[h]
9. An angel strengthened Jesus in Gethsemane before the cross.[i]
10. An angel rolled the stone away from Jesus' tomb.[k]
11. An angel told two women at the empty tomb that Jesus had risen.[m]
12. Two angels comforted Mary Magdalene and reunited her with Jesus.[n]
13. Angels promised that Jesus would be coming again.[o]

And still yet to come, angels will declare Jesus' victory and ride into history with Him for war in the end.[p]

[a] Luke 1:11-17 [b] Matt. 1:21; Luke 1:13 [c] Matt. 1:20-21; Luke 1:26-37 [d] Matt. 1:20-21 [e] Luke 2:8-15 [f] Luke 2:13-14 [g] Matt. 2:13, 20 [h] Matt. 4:11 [i] Luke 22:43 [k] Matt. 28:2 [m] Matt. 28:5–7; Luke 24:4–7; John 20:11–14 n John 20:11–1 [o] Acts 1:10-11 [p] Rev. 1:1; 19:9; 22:1, 6, 16

36. How did Jesus serve outcasts?*

The Samaritans were sexually confused, started a cult, and even sacrificed their children to demons who masqueraded as gods. While others walked around Samaria, God came to earth and went for a long walk to that very place. In the heat of the desert Jesus sat down at a well to have a conversation with a Samaritan woman, as John 4 reports. She was an outcast, married five times, and living with some guy who had taken advantage of her abused and confused state. Jesus was Jewish. The woman was Samaritan. Between these two groups was a war over worship.

In the days of Ezra and Nehemiah, the Jewish exiles who had returned to Jerusalem began repairing and rebuilding the temple so they could worship God there. The Samaritans offered to help but were told that as godless idolaters who did not possess salvation, their assistance was unwelcome. Sitting with Jesus, the Samaritan woman asked Jesus the theological issue dividing their religions, races, and worship: Where should she go to worship God? Jesus' answer changed the course of human history. Jesus declared an end to both Samaritan and Jewish worship, and instead favored worshipping in spirit and truth. Jesus speaks all this to a sole, sinful Samaritan woman. He knows her, and now she knows Him, so their eternal relationship begins. Stunned, she runs into town telling the good news of Jesus as one of the first and greatest evangelists in the entire New Testament, sparking a revival in Samaria.

37. What did Jesus say that no one else has said?@

1. Jesus said He was from Heaven and visited our planet, "I have come down from heaven".ᵃ
2. Jesus said He alone was the One True God, and was killed for this very reason, "because you...claim to be God".ᵇ No other religion has its founder declaring Himself to be God.
3. Jesus said He alone was completely sinless, inviting anyone to disprove his perfection saying, "Which of you can truthfully accuse me of one single sin?"ᶜ
4. Jesus said that He alone could forgive sin saying, "your sins are forgiven" which puzzled the religious leaders because THE problem God has with us is sin and, "Who can forgive sins but God alone?"ᵈ
5. Jesus promised to defeat death as proof that He is the only God, "he began to tell them about the terrible things he would suffer...and be killed, and that he would rise again three days afterwards."ᵉ
6. Jesus said He was the only way to Heaven, "I am the way and the truth and the life. No one comes to the Father except through me."ᶠ

ᵃ John 6:38 ᵇ John 10:33 ᶜ John 8:46 ᵈ Mark 2:5,7-8 ᵉ Mark 8:31 ᶠ John 14:6

5
QUESTIONS ABOUT WHAT JESUS TAUGHT

38. Does Jesus forbid us to not judge others?..............47
39. What did Jesus teach about homosexuality?...........48
40. How did Jesus speak about politics?..................49
41. Is Jesus the only way to Heaven?.....................50
42. How did Jesus view women?..........................51

38. Does Jesus forbid us from judging others?$

I'm sure you've heard Matthew 7:1: "Do not judge others, and you will not be judged." It seems to be the most popular verse that sinful Christians or confused non-Christians quote. Interpreting Scripture is like understanding a conversation. If you only catch a line or two in the middle, you can easily misunderstand. The key to understanding Jesus' teaching on judgment is to read the whole passage, verses 1-9 of Matthew 7.

In Matthew 7, Jesus rebukes religious leaders who condemn others for sins they tolerate in their own life. Jesus Himself judges them when He calls them hypocrites who have logs protruding from their eyes. He even calls some people "pigs," an extreme offense in a culture that considered pigs religious pollutants. A few verses later in Matthew 7:15, Jesus rails at "false prophets" who are "wolves," yet another stinging judgment. What Jesus forbid was not all judging but rather rash and hypocritical judging. That warning hits home for me. It was religious leaders who attacked Jesus the most viciously.

39. What did Jesus teach about homosexuality?[$]

Jesus was a rabbi—a teacher of the Old Testament. In His ancient Jewish context, homosexuality was universally seen as contrary to God's design. Jesus unabashedly grounded right sexual practice in the created order of Genesis 1–2. Robert Gagnon, who has likely done more scholarly work than anyone on the Bible and homosexuality, summarizes the evidence:

> "There is little historical doubt about Jesus' view of homo sexual practice. Although focused on the indissolubility of marriage, in Mark 10:5–9 he clearly presupposed that the presence of a 'male and female' was an important prerequisite of marriage (Gen. 1:27). Only a 'man' and a 'woman' are structurally capable of being 'joined' through a sexually intimate relationship into a one-flesh union (2:24)...For Jesus, then, the Creator ordained marriage—it was not just a social construct—as a lifelong union of one man and one woman. Both the Scriptures Jesus cited with approval and the audience addressed—indeed, the whole of early Judaism, so far as extant evidence indicates."[5&6]

He also argues that if Jesus had wanted His disciples to think otherwise, He would have had to state such a view clearly. As it is, we know of no dissenting opinions on the issue in earliest Christianity.

40. How did Jesus speak about politics?[$]

Whether you locate yourself on the political right, left, or in the middle, Jesus calls you to something more. If He were retelling His ancient parable of a couple lost sons today, the rebellious brother would lean politically left. The religious brother would lean politically right. The younger brother would march in a pride parade or a protest. The older brother would picket those parades and protest the protests. But notice this: Jesus doesn't join either brother on the right or the left. He also doesn't join the masses trying to duck the issues in the middle. Jesus is greater than politics. When the Roman prefect Pontius Pilate asked if He had revolutionary aspirations, Jesus replied, "My kingdom is not of this world".[a] Jesus the King rules over all kings, and His Kingdom reigns over all kingdoms. But the Kingdom of King Jesus has not yet come in its fullness, and until we see it we are to pray as He taught us: "Your kingdom come".[b] When the Kingdom of Jesus arrives, sin will be replaced with salvation, death with resurrection, sickness with healing, war with peace, poverty with prosperity, and tears with laughter. From the first day we meet Jesus, our citizenship in His Kingdom is secure, but until we arrive in Heaven we are stuck here. But that doesn't mean you're not meant to be here.

---

[a] John 18:36, NIV [b] Matt. 6:10

41. Is Jesus the only way to Heaven?[$]

Many Bible passages clarify the exclusive, all-important claims of Jesus regarding salvation. One of the most obvious is Luke 13:22–30. As Jesus taught His way through Israel's towns and villages, someone asked Him a question for the ages: "Lord, will those who are saved be few?".[a] Who will make it to Heaven? We learn a few things from this passage:

1. Salvation is one narrow door.
2. The narrow door is exclusive and inclusive.
3. The narrow door is closing.
4. The narrow door divides Heaven and Hell.
5. The narrow door IS Jesus.

[a] Luke 13:23, ESV

42. How did Jesus view women?$

Jesus was a revolutionary in His relationships with women. He was unafraid to break man-made cultural taboos, although He was careful never to transgress God's law. Jesus talked with the woman at the well and the widow of Nain.[a] He cast demons out of women and healed them.[b] He lifted up women as examples as He preached[c], and He taught women along with men, a highly controversial act in that day.[d] Jesus did not flinch when a sinful woman anointed Him and scandalized the religious guys who witnessed her devotion.[e] Jesus was close friends with Mary and Martha, women He loved like sisters who had Him over to eat in their home.[f] Women were among the most generous financial supporters of Jesus' ministry.[g] And women were granted the great honor of being the first to discover Jesus had risen.[h]

[a] Luke 7:12–13 [b] Matt. 9:20-22; Luke 8:40-56, 13:10-17 [c] Matt. 25:1-10; Luke 4:26, 18:1-5, 21:1-4 [d] Luke 10:38–42, 23:27–31; John 20:10–18 [e] Luke 7:36-50 [f] Luke 10:38-39 [g] Luke 8:1-3 [h] Matt. 28:1-10

3
QUESTIONS ABOUT JESUS' RELATIONSHIP WITH THE FATHER

43. How did Jesus pray to the Father?....................53
44. How did Jesus know the Father's will?................54
45. What attributes did Jesus share with the Father and Holy Spirit?..55

43. How did Jesus pray to the Father?[+]

A theological dictionary speaks of a term that Jesus uses most frequently when addressing His Father in prayer,

> "The teaching of the Fatherhood of God takes a decided turn with Jesus, for 'Father' was his favorite term for addressing God. It appears on his lips some sixty-five times in the Synoptic Gospels and over one hundred times in John. The exact term Jesus used is still found three times in the New Testament (Mark 14:36; Rom 8:15–16; Gal 4:6) but elsewhere the Aramaic term Abba is translated by the Greek pater....The uniqueness of Jesus' teaching on this subject is evident for several reasons. For one, the rarity of this designation for God is striking. There is no evidence in pre-Christian Jewish literature that Jews addressed God as 'Abba.' A second unique feature about Jesus' use of Abba as a designation for God involves the intimacy of the term. Abba was a term little children used when they addressed their fathers. At one time it was thought that since children used this term to address their fathers the nearest equivalent would be the English term 'Daddy.' More recently, however, it has been pointed out that Abba was a term not only that small children used to address their fathers; it was also a term that older children and adults used. As a result it is best to understand Abba as the equivalent of 'Father' rather than 'Daddy.'"[7]

44. How did Jesus know the Father's will?[+][*]

The Bible speaks of God as a Father. There are basically two kinds of dads. The red-light dad says no most of the time; has many rules; is controlling, domineering, and demanding; and as a result, is not very relational or fun. The green-light dad says yes most of the time; has only a few rules; is very freeing, encouraging, and helpful; and as a result, is very relational and a lot of fun. The God of the Bible is a green-light Dad and not a red-light Dad. He told Adam and Eve that all of creation was a green light and that "You may surely eat of every tree of the garden".[a]

Did you catch that? Everything was a green light (yes) with only one red light (no), "but of the tree of the knowledge of good and evil you shall not eat, for in the day that you eat of it you shall surely die." Our Father said yes to everything but one thing, and told us He forbade that action because it would hurt us. Dad wants us to live in freedom and joy. It is vital that you understand the identity of God as a loving, relational, helpful, safe, wise, green-light Dad. Do you? As a Christian you must base your identity upon two things, perhaps the most important things you can learn studying the Bible: (1) who God really is, and (2) who God says you really are. It is no surprise that demonic attack starts on those two fronts, with Satan giving a counterfeit identity for God and you. If you have a wrong view of God and/or who you are in relation to God, then everything in your life spins out of control, as it did for Adam and Eve.

[a] Gen. 2:16-17

45. What attributes did Jesus share with the Father and Holy Spirit?[?]

Omniscience: God has perfect knowledge of all things, including the past, present, future, and everything actual or potential.[a] It is comforting to know that God knows all about us, yet still loves and forgives us. Since God knows everything, nothing can separate us from Him, nothing can surprise Him, and He knows all our needs.

Omnipotence: God is all-powerful and able to do all that He wills.[b] It is God's power that guarantees assurance of our salvation.[c] Because of God's power over all else, we can trust God to work out our seemingly impossible situations for His glory and our good.[d]

Immutability: God does not change.[e] God is perfect and remains the same even when we change, and we can trust what God has said in Scripture because His Word never changes either.

Eternality: God has no beginning and no end and is not bound by time, although He created time, is conscious of time, and does work in time.[f] Because God sees things from an eternal perspective, He knows what is best for our lives and for the events that take place in the world.

Self-Existence: God is the only being who is not controlled by external forces and does not depend upon anyone or anything for His continued existence.ᵍ It is reassuring to know God is the Creator of all things and all things are dependent upon Him. Also, since God created us, He can sustain us and control our future for good.

Sovereignty: God is supreme in rule and authority over all thingsʰ, though He does allow human freedom as He wills.ⁱ No attribute can supply the security and comfort in terrible trials like God's sovereignty, because within our trials is the reminder that there is a God who is working out all things for our eventual good.ᵏ

Transcendence: God is fully distinct from the universe He created.ᵐ It is awe-inspiring and comforting to know the enormity and otherness of God and His infinite grandeur.

Creator: God brought all things into existence out of nothing, solely by His power.ⁿ It is a pleasure to enjoy God's creation, and also amazing to consider He created all that is out of nothing by the sheer power of Himself.

ᵃ Job 42:2; Pss. 139:1–6; 147:5; Isa. 40:12–14; 46:10; Heb. 4:13. ᵇ Job 42:2; Ps. 147:5; Matt. 19:26; Eph. 3:20. ᶜ Rom. 1:16; 8:35–39. ᵈ Gen. 18:14; Jer. 32:17, 27; Luke 1:37; Rom. 8:28 ᵉ Num. 23:19; Ps. 102:27; Mal. 3:6; Rom. 11:29; Heb. 13:8; James 1:17 f Ps. 90:2; 93:2; 102:12; Eph. 3:21 ᵍ Ex. 3:14; Isa. 41:4; 43:10; 44:6; 48:12; Rev. 1:8, 17; 2:8; 3:14; 21:6; 22:13 ʰ 2 Sam. 7:28; 1 Chron. 29:10–13; Ps. 103:19 ⁱ Gen. 50:20; Rom. 1:18–32 ᵏ Gen. 50:20; Rom. 8:28 ᵐ Gen. 1:1; Ps. 102:25-27; Isa. 42:5; Acts 17:24; 1 John 2:15-17 ⁿ Gen. 1:1; Ps. 33:6, 102:25; Isa. 44:24; John 1:3; Rom. 11:36; Heb. 1:2, 11:3

5

QUESTIONS ABOUT JESUS' RELATIONSHIP WITH THE HOLY SPIRIT

46. How did the Holy Spirit empower Jesus' prayer life?.....58
47. How did Jesus mature by the Holy Spirit?..............59
48. Why did the Holy Spirit show up at Jesus' baptism?.....60
49. How was Jesus' whole life led by the Holy Spirit?.......61
50. Why did Jesus need the Holy Spirit?..................63

46. How did the Holy Spirit empower Jesus' prayer life?[+]

In Luke 11:1, the disciples say to Jesus, "Lord teach us to pray," and Jesus responds in Luke 11:13, "If you then, who are evil, know how to give good gifts to your children, how much more will the heavenly Father give the Holy Spirit to those who ask him!" Jesus' answer to the request "Teach us to pray" is about receiving the gift of the Holy Spirit, because, while Trinitarian prayer is directed to the Father, it is empowered by the Holy Spirit. The Holy Spirit actually teaches us how to pray and Jesus himself prayed by the Spirit in Luke 10:21-22. This prayer of Jesus is described as "rejoicing in the Holy Spirit," indicating that the Son's prayer to the Father is conducted in the joyful power of the Holy Spirit. This is a beautiful description of worshipful prayer that shows us how the Spirit empowers us to pray.

47. How did Jesus mature by the Holy Spirit?=

For starters His name "Christ" literally means the one anointed with the person, presence, and power of the Holy Spirit. In the Old Testament we read about the boy Samuel maturing through the power of the Holy Spirit by growing up in the presence of God. In 1 Samuel 2:21 it says, "Indeed the Lord visited Hannah, and she conceived and bore three sons and two daughters. And the boy Samuel grew in the presence of the Lord." The Bible uses the same kind of language here as it does to explain Moses dwelling in the Spirit to such a degree that he has an intimate and personal transforming connection with God.[a] In 1 Samuel 2:26 it says, "Now the boy Samuel continued to grow both in stature and in favor with the Lord and also with man." Similar to Samuel, Luke 2:40 says of Jesus, "And the child grew and became strong, filled with wisdom. And the favor of God was upon him." Regarding His age, most Bible commentators agree that this refers to Jesus as a younger child under the age of twelve. In the following section of verses Luke 2:52 says, "Jesus increased in wisdom and in stature and in favor with God and man."

[a] Exod. 34:29–35 cf.; Num. 11:25

48. Why did the Holy Spirit show up at Jesus' baptism?

The baptism of Jesus Christ is so significant that it appears in all four of the New Testament Gospels. Luke 3:21–22 reports, "Now when all the people were baptized, and when Jesus also had been baptized and was praying, the heavens were opened, and the Holy Spirit descended on him in bodily form, like a dove; and a voice came from heaven, 'You are my beloved Son; with you I am well pleased.'"

This event was not Jesus receiving the Holy Spirit for the first time. In the previous chapters Luke clearly tells us that the Holy Spirit was intimately involved in the life and ministry of Jesus Christ from the womb. Mary, His mother, conceived Jesus by the power of the Holy Spirit. Therefore, at every moment of His journey into human history through the womb of Mary, the Spirit was present in power with Jesus. Jesus' baptism was not where He received the Spirit, but rather it was a public event where the Father "revealed" to the crowd what Jesus already knew—that He lived in loving and constant relationship with God the Father and God the Spirit.[a] This was crucially important because God's people had long awaited the fulfillment of Isaiah's promises that their Savior would come in the power of the Spirit.

---

[a] John 1:31

49. How was Jesus' whole life led by the Holy Spirit?[%]

The empowerment of Jesus by God the Holy Spirit is repeatedly stressed in the Gospel of Luke, which precedes Acts in showing the Spirit-filled life of Christ and then Christians as the two-part history of our faith. Here are a few examples:

1. Jesus was conceived by the Holy Spirit and given the title "Christ," which means anointed by the Holy Spirit.[a]

2. Jesus' relative Elizabeth was "filled with the Holy Spirit" when greeting Jesus' pregnant mother Mary, and her husband Zechariah went on to prophesy in the Spirit that their son John was appointed by God to prepare the way for Jesus.[b]

3. An angel revealed to Mary that she would give birth to Jesus because "the Holy Spirit will come upon you."[c]

4. Once born, Jesus was dedicated to the Lord in the temple according to the demands of the law by Simeon; "the Holy Spirit was upon [Simeon]" and the Holy Spirit had revealed to him that he would not die until seeing Jesus Christ.[d]

5. Simeon was "in the Spirit" when he prophesied about Jesus' ministry to Jews and Gentiles.[e]

6. John prophesied in the Spirit that one day Jesus would baptize people with the Holy Spirit.[f]

7. The Holy Spirit descended upon Jesus at His own baptism.[g] Matthew adds the interesting statement that the Spirit rested on Jesus, as if to suggest that the remainder of His life and ministry on the earth would be done under the anointing and power of the Holy Spirit.[h]

8. Jesus was "full of the Holy Spirit."[i]

9. Jesus was "led by the Spirit."[k]

10. Jesus came "in the power of the Spirit."[m]

11. After reading Isaiah 61:1–2, "The Spirit of the Lord GOD is upon me," Jesus declared, "Today this Scripture has been fulfilled in your hearing."[n]

12. Jesus "rejoiced in the Holy Spirit."[o]

---

[a] Luke 1-2 [b] Luke 1:41-43, 67, 76 [c] Luke 1:35-37 [d] Luke 2:25-27 [e] Luke 2:27-34 [f] Matt. 3:11; Mar. 1:8; Luke 3:16; John 1:34 [g] Matt. 3:16; John 1:32-33 [h] Matt. 3:16 [i] Luke 4:1-2 [k] Luke 4:1-2 [m] Luke 4:14 [n] Luke 4:14-21 [o] Luke 10:21

50. Why did Jesus need the Holy Spirit?=

Jesus relied on the Holy Spirit in many ways throughout His ministry, but one poignant example that we can glean from is in Luke 4. Like Moses[a] and Elijah[b], Jesus spent forty days alone in the wilderness.

By the time the dragon showed up for war, Jesus had reached the limits of His humanity. In this we learn when our Enemy is likely to HIT—when we are hungry, isolated, and tired.

When we are physically unwell and in need of food or some other provision, we are more open to temptation since we lack the energy we need to fight. When we are isolated because we live alone, have no close friends or family living nearby, and can live a life filled with secrecy because of privacy, we are also more vulnerable to sinful temptation. When we are tired, our energy levels are low because we are burned out, not sleeping well, sick, injured, overconsuming alcohol, using illegal drugs, or experiencing poor health for any reason, the Enemy sees us as wounded prey that he can more easily devour.

Living out of His full humanity, the Lord Jesus was vulnerable. We are as well, anytime we find ourselves hungry, isolated, or tired. Satan and demons are not limited by lack of sleep, sickness, or low energy levels, so Jesus relied on the Holy Spirit to maintain control over them at all times, as can we.

[a] Exod. 34:28 [b] 1 Kings 19:8

4

QUESTIONS ABOUT JESUS' BATTLE WITH THE DEMONIC

51. How did Satan attack Jesus?........................ 65
52. How did Jesus identify Satan's schemes?............. 66
53. How did Jesus defeat Satan on earth?............... 67
54. How did Jesus defeat Satan in Heaven?..............69

51. How did Satan attack Jesus?*

Not only did angels serve Jesus, but Satan's attack on Jesus also commenced when Jesus was only a boy. King Herod decreed that all firstborn sons be put to death in an effort to murder Jesus as an infant. Through an angel, God warned Jesus' parents of the plot, and they fled to Egypt as refugees to spare Jesus' life. Jesus was later attacked by Satan the tempter, who offered him a much easier life than the one planned for Him by God the Father. God sent Jesus to earth to live a sinless life and die on the cross for sinners. In contrast, Satan offered a kingdom without a cross and promised that Jesus could rule in glory and power without any opposition or crucifixion so long as He bowed down in honor to Satan. The backdrop of the entire life of Jesus is spiritual warfare. Leading up to the cross, Satan nearly got Peter to join the demonic rebellion, but Jesus prayed for him: "Simon, Simon, behold, Satan demanded to have you, that he might sift you like wheat, but I have prayed for you".[a] Satan will try and recruit you into his rebellion as well, but the good news is that Jesus continually prays for you as He "always lives to make intercession".[b] Judas Iscariot welcomed Satan[c] and conspired with him to betray Jesus and hand Him over to be crucified. All of this was spiritual warfare. Through the cross, Satan and his demons thought they had finally defeated Jesus. If we picture the Lord Jesus hanging on the cross, bloodied and dying, it looks like the devil has finally won. Isaiah 45:15 says, "Truly, you are a God who hides himself, O God of Israel, the Savior." On the cross, Jesus hid His victory in defeat, hid His glory in shame, and hid our life in His death.

[a] Luke 22:31-32 [b] Heb. 7:25 [c] John 13:27

52. How did Jesus identify Satan's schemes?*

Demonic forces frequently attack Christians in the area of their identity, but most of us are unaware of it. In the accounts of Adam and Jesus, there is an incredibly insightful clue. Like a poker player's "tell," Satan's subtle behavior is detectable if you watch for it, and it can alert you of his attack on your identity. When speaking to Adam, Jesus, and you, the demonic realm speaks in the second-person word "you". To Adam and Eve, Satan said, "You will not surely die" and "you will be like God." When speaking to Jesus, Satan said twice, "If you are the Son of God."

When you speak of yourself, you use the first-person pronoun "I." When someone else speaks to you, they use the second-person pronoun "you." When a physical being talks to us in the second person, we easily recognize that we are being spoken to by someone else. But when a spiritual being talks to us in the second person, we have to decide if we are hearing from God or the devil and his demons. Sometimes when a demon does speak to us, we can easily overlook the fact that we are being spoken to by a demon because they are unseen.

53. How did Jesus defeat Satan on earth?*

Our King Jesus said, "All authority in heaven and on earth has been given to me."[a] If you belong to Jesus Christ, you need to believe the following four things so you can exercise the authority He delegated to you as you wage your war.

1. You have moved from the kingdom of darkness to the kingdom of light. For Christians, this life is as close to Hell as we will ever be; it is as bad as it will ever get. Conversely, for non-Christians, this life is as close to Heaven as they will ever be; it is as good as it will ever get.

2. Demonic attack is not uncommon. Demonic attack is constant, often seducing the flesh within us because we are living in the midst of a war that has been raging since it erupted in Heaven. Knowing about this war can cause panic, but God invites you to cast "all your anxieties on him, because he cares for you. Be sober-minded; be watchful. Your adversary the devil prowls around like a roaring lion, seeking someone to devour. Resist him, firm in your faith, knowing that the same kinds of suffering are being experienced by your brotherhood throughout the world".[b]

3. You come with your King's authority. No one and nothing has authority equal to Jesus Christ. Today Jesus is at the right hand of the Father "seated...in the heavenly

places, far above all rule and authority and power and dominion, and above every name that is named, not only in this age but also in the one to come," with everyone and everything "under his feet".[c]

4. Your defeated enemy has to surrender to your victorious King. The Spirit of God in you is greater than the demonic spirits against you, and if you do not surrender to the demonic but instead surrender to God, they will also surrender to Him and leave you as they did Jesus.

---

[a] Matt. 28:18 [b] 1 Pet. 5:7-9 [c] Ephesians 1:15-22

54. How did Jesus defeat Satan in Heaven?*

Much like a commanding military officer that seeks to incite a coup to overthrow a king and overtake a kingdom, one of the highest-ranking spirit beings, also called the "strong man" or "prince of demons,"[a] became filled with pride.[b] We now know him by various names such as Satan, the devil, the evil one, the prince of the power of the air, the spirit of the world, Belial, the enemy, the adversary, the serpent, the dragon, the tempter, the god of this world, and the counterfeit spirit.[c] Rather than glorifying God, he wanted to be glorified as god. Rather than obeying God, he wanted to be obeyed as god. Rather than living dependently upon God, he wanted to live independently as his own god. Rather than building the Kingdom, he wanted to expand his own kingdom. The battlefield report from the unseen realm says, "Now war arose in heaven, Michael and his angels fighting against the dragon. And the dragon and his angels fought back, but he was defeated, and there was no longer any place for them in heaven. And the great dragon was thrown down, that ancient serpent, who is called the devil and Satan, the deceiver of the whole world—he was thrown down to the earth, and his angels were thrown down with him."[d]

---

[a] Matt. 4:8–9; 9:34; 12:24, 29; Mark 3:22–27; Luke 4:6; 11:21–22; John 12:31; 14:30; 16:11; 1 John 5:19 [b] Isa. 14:11–23; Ezek. 28:12 [c] Rom. 16:20; 1 Cor. 5:5; 7:5; 2 Cor. 2:11; 11:14; 12:7; 1 Thess. 2:18; 2 Thess. 2:9; 1 Tim. 1:20; 5:15; Eph. 4:27; 6:11; 1 Tim. 3:6–7; 2 Tim. 2:26; Eph. 6:16; 2 Thess. 3:3; Eph. 2:2; 2 Cor. 6:15; Luke 10:19; 1 Tim. 5:14; 2 Cor. 11:3; Rev. 12:9; 1 Thess. 3:5; 2 Cor. 4:4; 11:4 [d] Rev. 12:7-9

9

QUESTIONS ABOUT JESUS' BETRAYAL AND DEATH

55. What did Jesus do the night He was betrayed?........71
56. What did Jesus endure on the cross?..................72
57. How did Jesus die?...................................73
58. What did Jesus say on the cross?....................74
59 What is crucifixion?..................................75
60. How did Jesus predict His own death?................77
61. Where was Jesus buried?.............................78
62. How do we know Jesus actually died?................79
63. For whom did Jesus die?.............................80

55. What did Jesus do the night He was betrayed?[+]

As Jesus approached the end of His last day, He stopped to spend an entire night in prayer. What someone does in the final moments of their life reveals who or what they care most about. Jesus' actions reveal that meeting with the Father in prayer was His highest priority. Reading Jesus' Gethsemane Prayer is spiritually overwhelming, just as it was physically overwhelming for Jesus. His tear-stained agonizing prayer is a sacred glimpse into His most miserable moment so that He might comfort us on our darkest days. Gethsemane means an oil press, and an oil press stood amid a field of olive trees where it was used to press the oil from the fruit by crushing it. John 18:1 reveals that an olive grove, or garden, was in this place where Jesus prayed. There, Jesus' soul would be pressed until it was crushed, and heartfelt prayer poured forth. Jesus' prayer in the darkness of the garden is brutally and painfully honest. In His darkest hour of abandonment and betrayal, with the horrid specter of crucifixion quickly coming, Jesus did not doubt the Father, deny the Father, rebel against the Father, or run from the Father. No, instead, He got down on His knees in surrender to speak with the Father in prayer. In this act, we witness another reminder of one of the great truths about prayer: it is not primarily about getting God to do what we want, but rather about having our will aligned with His. That way, when the most brutal moments of life envelop us, we will take the Father's hand to lead us through—and not around—our valleys of darkness.

56. What did Jesus endure on the cross?

In mockery, a sign was posted above Jesus that said, "Jesus of Nazareth, the King of the Jews."[8] At this point during a crucifixion, the victims labored to breathe as their bodies went into shock. Naked and embarrassed, the victims would often use their remaining strength to seek revenge on the crowd of mockers who had gathered to jeer them. They would curse at their tormentors while urinating and spitting on them. Some victims would become so overwhelmed with pain that they would become incontinent and a pool of sweat, blood, urine, and feces would gather at the base of their cross. Crucifixion usually kills by asphyxiation in addition to other factors—the heart is deeply stressed, the body is traumatized, the muscles are devastated, and the blood loss is severe. Doctors have thought that Jesus likely had a chest contusion and possibly a bruised heart from falling with the cross on top of him, which caused an aneurysm.[9] Subsequently, Jesus' heart would have been unable to pump enough blood and his lungs would have filled up with carbon monoxide. Jesus not only lived through all of this, but he even spoke lucidly and clearly with enough volume to be heard by those present. Jesus hung on the cross for at least six hours—from the third hour to the ninth hour, when the darkness ended.[10] In accordance with the promise of Scripture, Jesus died quickly enough that his legs were not broken to speed up the process, as was customary.[11]

57. How did Jesus die?@

Jesus died by execution from the ancient Roman government. After being beaten beyond recognition for an entire night, Jesus carried a heavy wooden crossbar on His bloodied back. Jesus was then nailed to a cross through the most sensitive nerve centers on the body, His hands and feet. To ensure Jesus died, a soldier took a spear, ran it under His rib cage puncturing His heart sack so that water and blood flowed from His side. Jesus was dead. Jesus' dead body was then wrapped in upwards of a hundred pounds of burial linens and spices and laid in a cold tomb hewn out of rock without any medical attention for three days.

58. What did Jesus say on the cross?

From the cross Jesus announced forgiveness for those who crucified Him, assured the criminal crucified next to Him that they would be together in paradise, commended His mother to John, cried of forsakenness showing His spiritual death and separation from the Father, and expressed His agonized thirst.[12] At last Jesus said in a loud voice of triumph, "It is finished."[13] At this moment, the atonement for sin was made and the holiness, righteousness, justice, and wrath of the triune God were satisfied in the crucifixion of Jesus Christ. Jesus then said, "Father, into your hands I commit my spirit!"[14] Jesus reserved His final breath from the cross to shout His triumphant victory to the world by confirming that He had been restored to God the Father after atoning for human sin.

59. What is crucifixion?@

Imagine a long wooden stake being run through a person's midsection, and that stake then being driven into the ground, with the impaled person left to die slowly over the course of many days. This barbarous torture from the 9th century BC may be the earliest form of crucifixion.

The transition from impalement to crucifixion occurred under Alexander in the 4th century BC as he was a master of terror and dread. In the 1st century BC, the former gladiator Spartacus fell in battle to the Romans, resulting in six thousand men being crucified along the shoulder of the highway on a single day.

The Romans perfected crucifixion, reserving it as the most painful mode of execution for the most despised people. The crucifixion methods varied with the sadism of the soldiers, as they tried to outdo one another, experimenting with torture to prolong pain and agony. The Romans are believed to be the first to crucify on an actual cross. The Tau was a capital T cross and the Latin was a lowercase t cross. Both had the stipe (the vertical post) and patibulum (the crossbar). The stipe was probably permanent while each man carried his own patibulum.

The pain of crucifixion is so horrendous that a word was invented to explain it—excruciating—which literally means "from the cross." Crucifixion was painfully slow death by asphyxiation for the crucified, passing in and out of consciousness often for days on end. None of this was done in privacy, but rather in public places. It would be like nailing a bloodied, naked man above the front entrance to your local mall as state sponsored terror. People were likely crucified at eye level, looking their mockers in the face as they sweat in the sun, bled, and became incontinent from the pain. Crucifixion was the most painful and shameful way to die. God's people considered crucified people cursed, "If someone guilty of a capital offense is put to death...you must not leave the body hanging on the pole overnight...because anyone who is hung on a pole is under God's curse."[a]

---

[a] Deuteronomy 21:22-23

60. How did Jesus predict His own death?@

Throughout His earthly ministry, Jesus predicted His own death many times in an attempt to prepare His followers and disciples. Here are a few instances:

> Mark 9:31 - "I, the Messiah, am going to be betrayed and killed and three days later I will return to life again."
>
> Mark 10:33–34 - "I, the Messiah, will be arrested and taken before the chief priests and the Jewish leaders, who will sentence me to die and hand me over to the Romans to be killed. They will mock me and spit on me and flog me with their whips and kill me; but after three days I will come back to life again."

61. Where was Jesus buried?@

When a beloved person dies, we mark their graves to honor them. When a prophet or holy person dies, a shrine is made for their followers to visit. Of the four major world religions based upon a founder, only Christianity lacks a known grave or shrine. Abraham's Jewish holy site is at Hebron. Buddha's holy site is in India. Mohammed's Islamic holy site is in Medina. Each of these graves are visited by millions of people every year. Scholars have also found the tombs of at least 50 religious leaders enshrined in Jesus' day, but no sign of Jesus' burial place. No one knows where Jesus was buried, because He's no longer dead. Instead, He walked away from His tomb. According to former professor at the University of Durham James D. G. Dunn, there is "absolutely no trace" of any veneration at Jesus' tomb.[15]

62. How do we know Jesus actually died?@

To ensure Jesus was dead, a military executioner ran a spear through Jesus' side, which punctured His heart sac, and water and blood flowed from His side. This is evidence that Jesus died of a heart attack; the sac around the heart filled with water until the pressure caused Jesus' heart to stop beating. Jesus died with both a literal and metaphorical broken heart. On the cross, Jesus took your place and put you in His place. He died, so that you could live. He was cursed, so you could be blessed. He was separated from the Father, so you could be reconciled to the Father. All of this was done to Jesus, but for you, "God made Christ, who never sinned, to be the offering for our sin, so that we could be made right with God through Christ".[a] Jesus' dead body was then wrapped in upwards of a hundred pounds of burial linens and spices and laid in a cold tomb hewn out of rock without any medical attention for three days.

[a] 2 Corinthians 5:21

63. For whom did Jesus die?[%]

At the cross, justice and mercy kiss; Jesus substituted Himself for sinners and suffered and died in their place to forgive them, love them, and embrace them, not in spite of their sins, but because their sins were propitiated and diverted from them to Jesus. Jesus did this not by demanding our blood but rather by giving His own. The truth is that everyone but the sinless Jesus merits the active wrath of God. None of us deserves love, grace, or mercy from God. Demons and sinful people who fail to repent will have God's wrath burning against them forever. The place of God's unending active wrath is Hell. However, God's active wrath is diverted from some people because of the mercy of God. This is made possible because on the cross Jesus substituted Himself in our place for our sins and appeased God's righteous wrath. Two sections of Scripture in particular speak to this matter pointedly:

1. Romans 5:9: Since, therefore, we have now been justified by his blood, much more shall we be saved by him [Jesus] from the wrath of God.

2. 1 Thessalonians 1:9-10: You turned to God from idols to serve the living and true God, and to wait for his Son from heaven, whom he raised from the dead, Jesus who delivers us from the wrath to come.

Scripture also has a single word to designate how Jesus diverts the active wrath of our rightfully angry God from us so that we are loved and not hated. That word is propitiation, which summarizes more than six hundred related words and events that explain it. The "American Heritage Dictionary" defines propitiation as something that appeases or conciliates an offended power, especially a sacrificial offering to a god. Propitiate is the only English word that carries the idea of pacifying wrath by taking care of the penalty for the offense that caused the wrath.

10
QUESTIONS ABOUT JESUS' RESURRECTION

64. What is resurrection?............................... 83
65. Who found Jesus' empty tomb?..................... 84
66. What happened to Jesus' followers when He was resurrected?... 85
67. Who saw Jesus after He resurrected?................ 86
68. Where is Jesus' tomb?.............................. 87
69. How did the early church respond to the resurrection?... 88
70. Why can we trust the written accounts of Jesus' resurrection?... 89
71. What is the Biblical evidence for Jesus' resurrection?.....90
72. What historical evidence is there for Jesus' resurrection?.. 91
73. What is the circumstantial evidence for Jesus' resurrection?... 93

64. What is resurrection?[@]

The stories of near-death experiences, or of people who were pronounced dead coming back to life are revivifications, not resurrections, because those people eventually die again. Jesus' resurrection, which is the pattern for our resurrection, means to die, return from death, and defeat death to never die again, living an eternal life with your body and soul reunited forever. In the most scholarly book ever written on resurrection, "The Resurrection of the Son of God", N. T. Wright proves that in the first century, resurrection did not mean "life after death" in the sense of "the life that follows immediately after bodily death." Instead, "'Resurrection' denoted a new embodied life which would follow whatever 'life after death' there might be. 'Resurrection' was, by definition, not the existence into which someone might (or might not) go immediately upon death; it was not a disembodied 'heavenly' life; it was a further stage, out beyond all that. It was not a redescription or redefinition of death. It was death's reversal."[16]

65. Who found Jesus' empty tomb?@

Jesus' empty tomb was found by women. If the historical record of the Bible were fiction and not fact, women would not have been fabricated as the first eyewitnesses to the empty tomb, because their testimony was not as credible in court. Because these women honored their Lord, the Lord honored their testimony:

> "...on the first day of the week [Sunday], at early dawn, they went to the tomb...And they found the stone rolled away from the tomb, but when they went in they did not find the body of the Lord Jesus...it was Mary Magdalene and Joanna and Mary the mother of James and the other women with them...".[a]

[a] Luke 24:1-3,10

66. What happened to Jesus' followers when He resurrected?@

Jesus' disciples were transformed from cowards to courageous. Prior to Jesus' resurrection, His disciples were cowards with Peter denying Him, and Thomas doubting Him. Both men later died for Jesus as martyrs, along with other disciples, because they no longer feared death.

John 20:24-28 reports this transformation from cowards to courageous, "Thomas, one of the twelve...was not with them when Jesus came. So the other disciples told him, 'We have seen the Lord.' But he said to them, 'Unless I see in his hands the mark of the nails, and place my finger into the mark of the nails, and place my hand into his side, I will never believe.' Eight days later...Jesus came and stood among them and said, 'Peace be with you.' Then he said to Thomas, 'Put your finger here, and see my hands; and put out your hand, and place it in my side. Do not disbelieve, but believe.' Thomas answered him, 'My Lord and my God!'".

67. Who saw Jesus after He resurrected?[@]

After Jesus rose from death, He appeared to crowds upwards of 500 people over the course of 40 days. Jesus was available in His risen body to meet and talk with people following His resurrection, "For forty days after his death he appeared to them many times in ways that proved beyond doubt that he was alive. They saw him, and he talked with them...".[a] Jesus' resurrection was so wellknown that large crowds came to Him after He defeated death, "I delivered to you as of first importance...Christ died for our sins in accordance with the Scriptures, that he was buried, that he was raised on the third day in accordance with the Scriptures, and that he appeared to Cephas, then to the twelve. Then he appeared to more than five hundred brothers at one time, most of whom are still alive, though some have fallen asleep [died]."[b]

[a] Acts 1:3 [b] 1 Cor. 15:3-6

68. Where is Jesus' tomb?[@]

Jesus' tomb location was well-known. Some 700 years before Jesus was born, God promised that Jesus would be assigned a grave "with a rich man in his death."[a] This was incredibly unlikely, because Jesus was a very poor man who could not have afforded an expensive burial plot. This prophecy was fulfilled when, "a rich man from Arimathea, named Joseph...was a disciple of Jesus...And Joseph took the body and wrapped it in a clean linen shroud and laid it in his own new tomb, which he had cut in the rock. And he rolled a great stone to the entrance of the tomb and went away".[b] Jesus' tomb was easy to find because it belonged to a well-known affluent man who was still alive and legally owned it.

[a] Isaiah 53:9 [b] Matthew 27:57-60

69. How did the early church respond to the resurrection?@

The early church stopped worshiping on Saturday, as Jews had for thousands of years, and suddenly began worshiping on Sunday in memory of Jesus' Sunday resurrection.[a] The Jewish seven-day week with a Saturday Sabbath was established by God at creation. The Sabbath was so sacred to the Jews that they would not have ceased to obey one of the Ten Commandments unless Jesus had resurrected in fulfillment of their Old Testament Scriptures. Yet, by the end of the first century, Sunday was called "the Lord's Day".[b] To change the Sabbath was an attempt to literally reset the entire week, change their days of work and rest, and alter the business and worship dealings of the entire nation around Jesus' resurrection. God's people welcomed the sacraments of baptism and communion into their worship of Jesus as God. In communion, the early Christians remembered Jesus' death in their place for their sins. In baptism they remembered Jesus' resurrection in their place for their salvation and anticipated their personal future resurrection. These ancient practices have continued for thousands of years wherever the Church has existed.

[a] Acts 20:7; 1 Corinthians 16:1-2 [b] Revelation 1:10

70. Why can we trust the written accounts of Jesus' resurrection?[@]

Jesus' resurrection was recorded shortly after it occurred. Mark's Gospel account of the days leading up to Jesus' crucifixion mentions the high priest without naming him because he expected his readers to know who he was speaking of.[a] Since Caiaphas was high priest from AD 18–37, the latest possible date for the mention is AD 37, which is within a few short years of Jesus' death when eyewitnesses were still alive.

Jesus' resurrection was celebrated in the earliest church creeds. In 1 Corinthians 15:3-4, Paul says, "Christ died for our sins in accordance with the Scriptures, that he was buried, that he was raised on the third day in accordance with the Scriptures." This statement is widely accepted as the earliest church creed, which began circulating as early as AD 30-36, shortly after Jesus' resurrection. These facts prove that there was not sufficient time between the crucifixion and the report of Jesus' resurrection for a myth to become popular. In addition, the resurrection eyewitnesses were still alive and available to be questioned about the facts surrounding the resurrection.

[a] Mark 14:53, 54, 60, 61, 63

71. What is the Biblical evidence for Jesus' resurrection?

The biblical evidence for Jesus' resurrection is compelling and can be briefly summarized in 10 points. Each of these points is consistent, and together they reveal that the Bible is emphatically and repeatedly clear on the fact of Jesus' resurrection.

1. Jesus' resurrection was prophesied in advance.
2. Jesus predicted His own resurrection.
3. Jesus died.
4. Jesus was buried.
5. Jesus appeared physically alive three days after His death.
6. Jesus' resurrected body was the same as His pre-resurrection body.
7. Jesus' resurrection was recorded as Scripture shortly after it occurred.
8. Jesus' resurrection was celebrated in the earliest church creeds.
9. Jesus' resurrection convinced His family to worship Him as God.
10. Jesus' resurrection was confirmed by His most bitter enemies, such as Paul.

72. What historical evidence is there for Jesus' resurrection?[%]

Because Jesus' death is a historical fact, the corroborating evidence of non- Christian sources in addition to the Bible, helps to confirm the resurrection of Jesus Christ. The following testimony of Romans, Greeks, and Jews is helpful because these men are simply telling the facts without any religious devotion to them.

Josephus (AD 37–100)
Josephus was a Jewish historian born just a few years after Jesus died. His most celebrated passage, called the "Testimonium Flavianum," says:

> "Now there was about this time Jesus...He was [the] Christ. And when Pilate, at the suggestion of the principal men among us, had condemned him to the cross, those that loved him at the first did not forsake him; for he appeared to them alive again the third day, as the divine prophets had foretold these and ten thousand other wonderful things concerning him."[17]

Suetonius (AD 70–160)
Suetonius was a Roman historian and annalist of the Imperial House. In his biography of Nero (Nero ruled AD 54–68), Suetonius mentions the persecution of Christians by indirectly referring to the resurrection: "Punishment was inflicted on the

Christians, a class of men given to a new and mischievous superstition [the resurrection]."[18]

Pliny the Younger (AD 61 or 62–113)
Pliny the Younger wrote a letter to the emperor Trajan around AD 111 describing early Christian worship gatherings that met early on Sunday mornings in memory of Jesus' resurrection day:

"I have never been present at an examination of Christians... they had met regularly before dawn on a fixed day [Sunday in remembrance of Jesus' resurrection] to chant verses alternately amongst themselves in honor of Christ as if to a god."[19]

73. What is the circumstantial evidence for Jesus' resurrection?

Effects have causes. Jesus' resurrection is no exception, as is evident by eight effects caused by it. Together, they are compelling circumstantial evidence for Jesus' resurrection. Further, for those wanting to deny Jesus' resurrection, the burden of proof remains on them to account for these multiple effects with a reasonable cause.

1. Jesus' disciples were transformed.
2. Jesus' disciples remained loyal to Jesus as their victorious Messiah.
3. The disciples had exemplary character.
4. Worship changed from Saturday to Sunday.
5. Women discovered the empty tomb, although they couldn't testify in court, so fabricating a story with their story would have been ineffective.
6. The entirety of the early church preaching was centered around the resurrection.
7. Jesus' tomb was not enshrined.
8. Christianity exploded on the earth and a few billion people today claim to be Christians.

6
QUESTIONS ABOUT HOW PEOPLE KNEW JESUS WAS COMING

74. How was Jesus the fulfillment of the temple?. 95
75. What do the Psalms say about Jesus?. 97
76. What does Isaiah say about Jesus?. 98
77. What does Micah say about Jesus?. 99
78. What does Malachi say about Jesus?. 100
79. How is Jesus the hero of the whole Bible?. 101

74. How was Jesus the fulfillment of the temple?#

Jesus' visit to the temple represented a new epoch in human history. When Jesus and the temple come together, we see the fulfillment of the Old Covenant and the inauguration of the New Covenant taking place.

1. The temple was the connecting place between heaven and earth. God is in heaven as Creator, we are on earth as created, and God's very presence dwelt in the temple, in the Holy of Holies, making it the most sacred place on earth. Jesus came to connect the two realms.

2. The temple was the place of God's presence. In the Old Testament, if you wanted to be near God, you had to go to the temple. Now we can go to Jesus Himself as our Great High Priest and mediator.

3. The temple was where God's people would come to meet with him. We no longer need a place to meet God. We can talk to Jesus whenever we want.

4. The temple was the place where sin was atoned for. Priests would perform sacrifices, but Jesus was the ultimate sacrifice, atoning for sin once and for all.

5. The temple was the center of life and faith and worship. Four-hundred years before Jesus' birth, the prophet Malachi prophesied that the Messiah would come to the temple. The temple was destroyed in 70 A.D., just like Jesus said it would be.[a] Why? We have no need of it any longer. It has served its purpose. For hundreds of years, the temple prepared people for the coming of Jesus. And then He came.

---

[a] Matthew 26:61; Mark 14:58; John 2:19

75. What do the Psalms say about Jesus?@

Psalm 16:10 tells us: "For you will not abandon my soul to Sheol, or let your holy one see corruption." This was written in 1000 B.C. The Bible said that one person would be Holy. The one who would be Holy is Jesus Christ. And that though He would die, hH would rise and His body would not be left in the grave. This was promised a thousand years in advance.

76. What does Isaiah say about Jesus?@

I know that right now we're all suffering in a multitude of ways. For some of you, this suffering that you're experiencing right now is very intense. And let me say that Jesus is the God who relates to you, that Jesus is the God who comforts you, that Jesus is the God who sympathizes with you.

At the end of the Old Testament book of Isaiah, Jesus has promised to come as the suffering servant. And one of the ways that He serves us is through His suffering. Isaiah 53:7-11 says, "He was oppressed, and he was afflicted, yet he opened not his mouth; like a lamb that is led to the slaughter, and like a sheep that before its shearers is silent, so he opened not his mouth. By oppression and judgment he was taken away; and as for his generation, who considered that he was cut off out of the land of the living, stricken for the transgression of my people? And they made his grave with the wicked and with a rich man in his death, although he had done no violence, and there was no deceit in his mouth. Yet it was the will of the Lord to crush him; he has put him to grief; when his soul makes an offering for guilt, he shall see his offspring; he shall prolong his days; the will of the Lord shall prosper in his hand. Out of the anguish of his soul he shall see and be satisfied; by his knowledge shall the righteous one, my servant, make many to be accounted righteous, and he shall bear their iniquities."

77. What does Micah say about Jesus?

Seven hundred years before the birth of Jesus, Micah promised that Jesus would be born in Bethlehem: "But you, O Bethlehem Ephrathah, who are too little to be among the clans of Judah, from you shall come forth for me one who is to be ruler in Israel, whose coming forth is from of old, from ancient days".[a]

---

[a] Micah 5:2

78. What does Malachi say about Jesus?

Four hundred years before the birth of Jesus, Malachi promised that Jesus would enter the temple. Since the temple was destroyed in AD 70, this prophecy could not be fulfilled any time after AD 70. Malachi 3:1 tells us, "Behold, I send my messenger, and he will prepare the way before me. And the Lord whom you seek will suddenly come to his temple; and the messenger of the covenant in whom you delight, behold, he is coming, says the Lord of hosts."

79. How is Jesus the hero of the whole Bible?[%]

The opening line of Scripture introduces us to its Hero, God, who is revealed throughout the rest of the pages of Scripture. The Old and New Testament are about Jesus Christ – anyone can read the Bible, but only someone who reads it in the Spirit comes to this rightful conclusion. Some prefer the New Testament to the Old Testament because they wrongly believe that only the New Testament is about Jesus.

However, Jesus Himself taught that the Old Testament was primarily about Him while arguing with the theologians in his day. In John 5:39-40 Jesus says, "You search the Scriptures [Old Testament] because you think that in them you have eternal life; and it is they that bear witness about me, yet you refuse to come to me that you may have life."

The Bible is not just principles to live by, but a Person to live with. The Old Testament predicts the coming of Jesus in a variety of ways to prepare people. The Old Testament uses various means to reveal Jesus, including promises, appearances, foreshadowing types, and titles. The New Testament reflects back on the life of Jesus, particularly in the four Gospels, and reports the results of Jesus' life and ministry, particularly in the Epistles.

6
QUESTIONS ABOUT WHAT JESUS IS DOING RIGHT NOW

80. Where did Jesus say He was going?...................103
81. Where is Jesus right now?..........................104
82. How far does Jesus' rule extend right now?......... 105
83. What is Jesus doing for you right now?..............106
84. How is Jesus' power available to you right now?.....107
85. What is Jesus' relationship to the Church?..........108

80. Where did Jesus say He was going?

Before He was crucified, Jesus said in John 16:28, "I came from the Father and have come into the world, and now I am leaving the world and going to the Father." He told us exactly what He would be doing and how He would be operating. Jesus lived in glory for all eternity.

Isaiah says, "I saw the Lord high and exalted, seated upon the throne, surrounded by angels and divine beings who are crying out, "'Holy holy, holy is the Lord God Almighty.'" Then He came down to Earth in humility. He goes from hearing worship to hearing false accusations. He goes from hearing "holy, holy, holy" to hearing "crucify him, crucify him, crucify him". He goes from a throne in heaven to a manger on the earth. He goes from wealth to poverty. He goes from being served by angels to washing the feet of Judas Iscariot, His betrayer and pretend friend. This is Jesus in His humility. He went from glory to humility, to identify with you and me. After His death, burial, resurrection, He returns into heaven where He is ruling and reigning in glory.

81. Where is Jesus right now?

It was promised about a thousand years before Jesus even walked the earth in Psalm 110:1, "The Lord," that is God, the Father, "Says to my Lord," that is Jesus Christ, "Sit at my right hand until I make your enemies a footstool "under your feet." This is saying that Jesus uses His enemies as a footstool, which is awesome.

God the Father and God the Son are ruling and reigning, and the Father tells the Son He will be sent to defeat His enemies and return to rest His feet on them while sitting on a throne at the right hand of the Father. This is one of my favorite images in the whole Bible.

The throne is one of the centerpieces of the entire Bible. There's a thing called the divine council: God the Father, Son, and Spirit with His angelic and other divine beings, ruling and reigning. The center of the divine council is a throne, which tells us that the Father sits on a throne and that the Son sits at the right hand of the Father. That's the seat of power; that's the seat of authority, and He's sitting there right now.

82. How far does Jesus' rule extend right now?

When He was on the earth, Jesus said, "All things have been committed to Me by My Father" in Matthew 11:27. The Father has all authority, as does Jesus, as the Son of God, ruling and reigning from the right hand of the Father in glory and power. All peoples, times, places, religion, spiritualities, ideologies and philosophies are under the authority of Jesus. The highest authority is the authority of God. There is no one equal to God; there is no one over God. When Jesus is at the end of His life, He says, "All authority has been given to Me." He also said in John 3:35, "The Father loves the Son "and has placed everything in His hands." Everyone, everything, everyone and everything is under Jesus' jurisdiction right now. Ultimately, everyone and everything will give an account to Jesus on His throne.

83. What is Jesus doing for you right now?

First of all, Jesus is right now building you a home in Heaven. Whomever you are, however God made you, Jesus knows you, and He's custom-building an environment in the Father's house where you will feel loved and blessed and that is prepared for you. That's what He's doing right now. It gives us something to look forward to.

In addition, He is mediating for you. There is one mediator between God and man. It's not karma, good works, or enlightenment. It's Jesus. Because He's fully God and fully man, he can reconcile and mediate between men and God. The Bible teaches that Jesus comes down. God's the one that closes the gap. He talks to the Father about you and sends the Spirit to be with you.

84. How is Jesus' power available to you right now?

If Jesus is in Heaven and He has all power and all authority, wouldn't it be nice if you had access to some of that? And you do, through the Holy Spirit. In Acts 1:8-9, Jesus says, "You will receive power when the Holy Spirit has come upon you." Jesus goes up to Heaven and the Holy Spirit comes down. Just as we looked at the fact that Jesus was filled and led and empowered by the Spirit, He sends the Holy Spirit so that we would have access to the power that propelled His life in ministry to continue His message in ministry.

The Holy Spirit doesn't make you weird. He makes you like Jesus. The Jesus life is not just one to admire, but to experience. And if Jesus needed help from the Helper, imagine how much more help we need. Jesus lived by the person, the presence, the power of the Holy Spirit in His humility on the earth. And He sends the Holy Spirit to empower you and I to believe in His message and to continue His ministry.

85. What is Jesus' relationship to the Church?

- The head of the Church.[a] He is supreme. He is prominent. He is preeminent.
- The apostle who plants a church.[b] There is no church that comes into existence apart from Him. Those who are caught up in the hard work of church planting must always remember that Jesus is the apostle. While we can start an organization, only He can plant a church.
- The leader who builds the Church.[c] Ministry leaders go to work with Him, but unless He shows up, a church will not be built.
- The Chief Shepherd who rules the Church.[d] The Bible is clear that all the other pastors and leaders in churches are supposed to work under His leadership following His teaching and extending His mission.
- Present with the Church.[e] Jesus is the one who says, "I am with you always." In his exaltation, and through the Spirit, He is with us[f] and we are in Him.[g]
- The judge of the Church.[h] Since churches belong to Jesus, He has the authority to judge them, scatter them, close them, or whatever else He wants for whatever reasons He decides.

---

[a] Eph. 1:22; 4:15; 5:23 [b] Heb. 3:1 [c] Matt. 16:18 [d] 1 Pet. 5:4 [e] Matt. 28:18-20 [f] Col. 1:27 [g] John 17:21; Rom. 8:1; 1 Cor. 1:30; 2 Cor. 5:17; Phil. 3:9 [h] Rev. 2:5

APPENDIX
The Most Important Question of All: Do you Know Jesus?

Thank you of giving me the honor of helping you learn about Jesus Christ. It has been my hope in this book to help you learn more about Him. I grew up knowing a bit about Jesus, but did not personally know Jesus. I had a lot of questions about who He was, what He taught, how He lived, and if He, in fact, rose from death. Some friends were kind enough to answer my questions and help me receive Jesus Christ as my personal Lord and Savior. Jesus is the most important person in my life, and without Him everything in my life would be worse.

My prayer for you is that you would be a Christian and have a personal relationship with Jesus Christ. Having studied the most common and critical questions about Jesus, there is one question that He has for you, "Who do you say that I am?"[a]

Because Jesus is the most significant and influential person in world history, and the only founder of any major religion to say He was God, come down from Heaven, perfect without sin, the only way to eternal life in Heaven, and defeater of death, answering His question, "Who do you say that I am?" is the most important decision you will ever make.

[a] Matt. 16:15

British author C. S. Lewis (1898–1963) has said: "A man who was merely a man and said the sort of things Jesus said would not be a great moral teacher. He would either be a lunatic—on the level with the man who says he is a poached egg—or else he would be the Devil of Hell. You must make your choice. Either this man was, and is, the Son of God; or else a madman or something worse. You can shut Him up for a fool, you can spit at Him and kill Him as a demon; or you can fall at His feet and call Him Lord and God. But let us not come with any patronizing nonsense about His being a great human teacher. He has not left that open to us. He did not intend to."[20]

Liar?

If Jesus was a liar, He is the worst person who has ever lived. The entire Christian Church that is the largest, longest standing, and most diverse movement in world history is a fraud putting their hope in a man who has deceived them.

Lunatic?

If Jesus were a lunatic and delusional madman we should not honor or esteem Him. If His life and teachings were the result of mental health problems, we should have compassion for Him but not follow Him.

Lord?

If Jesus is Lord over all as God and Savior, we should turn from our sin, trust in Him, and live the rest of our life as Christians becoming more like Christ.

Who do you say that Jesus is? If you have not yet become a Christian and would like to, start by praying this prayer by simply speaking it aloud to God like you would have a conversation with a friend:

"Dear Jesus, I believe that I am a sinner who has done wrong in my thoughts, words, and deeds. I believe that you are God who came to earth to die for my sins and rise for my salvation. Please forgive me for my sins and make me a Christian. I commit to following your leadership for the rest of my life. I commit to listening to you in the Bible, speaking to you in prayer, and getting to know other Christian brothers and sisters in a local church. Amen!"

If you want to share your decision with us so we can pray for you, we would love to hear from you at hello@realfaith.com. If you have any prayer requests, need to find a good Bible that you can read, or have any other questions about Christ or Christianity, please contact us so we can pray for and serve you. Jesus loves you and I do too!

Pastor Mark Driscoll

ADDITIONAL RESOURCES
from Pastor Mark Driscoll

@ - Alive: 21 Reasons to Believe in the Resurrection of Jesus Christ (2021)

- The Boy Who is Lord: A Brief and Simple Look at the Birth and Childhood of Jesus. (2017)

$ - Christians Might Be Crazy: Answering the Top 7 Objections to Christianity (2018)

% - Doctrine (2021)

& - Faith Works: A Study in James (2021)

+ - Pray Like Jesus (2021)

= - Spirit-Filled Jesus: Live By His Power (2018)

! - Vintage Jesus: Timeless Answers to Timely Questions (2008)

? - Who is God?: A Brief and Simple Look at Who God is Through the Lens of Philosophy and Theology. (2015)

* - Win Your War: Fight in the Realm You Don't See for Freedom in the One You Do (2019)

*Find these resources referenced throughout this book by the corresponding symbols.

END NOTES

1. Dallas Theological Seminary (2004; 2005). Bibliotheca Sacra, vol. 161 (vnp.161.641.75)

2. Flavius Josephus, "Jewish Antiquities," in The New Complete Works of Josephus, trans. William Whiston (Grand Rapids, MI: Kregel, 1999), 18.63–64, emphasis added. There is great controversy about the authenticity of this text. Kostenberger, Andreas J.; Kellum, L. Scott; Quarles, Charles L. (2009). The Cradle, the Cross, and the Crown: An Introduction to the New Testament, pp. 104-108 is an excellent summary of the controversy.

3. Suetonius, Vita Nero 16.11-13

4. Pliny the Younger, Letters 10.96.1–7

5. Robert A. J. Gagnon, The Bible and Homosexual Practice: Texts and Hermeneutics (Nashville: Abingdon, 2002), 159–83.

6. Robert A. J. Gagnon, "Sexuality," in Dictionary for Theological Interpretation of the Bible, ed. Kevin J. Vanhoozer (Grand Rapids: Baker, 2005), 745.

7. Robert H. Stein, "Fatherhood of God," Evangelical Dictionary of Biblical Theology, Baker Reference Library (Grand Rapids, MI: Baker Book House, 1996), 247, https://www.biblestudytools.com/dictionaries/ bakers-evangelical-dictionary/fatherhood-of-god.html.

8 Aeschylus, Eumenides 647–48, quoted in Wright, Resurrection, 32.

9. Wright, Resurrection, 35.

10. Ibid., 76

11. Ibid., 81–82.

12. Wright, Resurrection, 53.

13. Ibid.

14. Ibid., 60.

15. James D. G. Dunn, The Christ and the Spirit (Grand Rapids, MI: Eerdmans, 1998), 67–68.

16. N. T. Wright, The Resurrection of the Son of God (Minneapolis: Fortress Press, 2003), 30–31.

17. Flavius Josephus, "Jewish Antiquities," in The New Complete Works of Josephus, trans. William Whiston (Grand Rapids, MI: Kregel, 1999), 18.63–64, emphasis added. There is great controversy about the authenticity of this text. Kostenberger, Andreas J.; Kellum, L. Scott; Quarles, Charles L. (2009). The Cradle, the Cross, and the Crown: An Introduction to the New Testament, pp. 104-108 is an excellent summary of the controversy.

18. Suetonius, Vita Nero 16.11–13.

19. Pliny the Younger, Letters 10.96.1–7.

20. C. S. Lewis, Mere Christianity (New York: Macmillan, 1952), 40–41.

IT'S ALL ABOUT JESUS!

realfaith.com

ABOUT PASTOR MARK DRISCOLL & REALFAITH

With Pastor Mark, it's all about Jesus! He is a spiritual leader, prolific author, and compelling speaker, but at his core, he is a family man. Mark and his wife Grace have been married and doing vocational ministry together since 1993 and, along with their five kids, planted Trinity Church in Scottsdale, Arizona as a family ministry.

Pastor Mark, Grace, and their oldest daughter, Ashley, also started RealFaith Ministries, which contains a mountain of Bible teaching for men, women, couples, parents, pastors, leaders, Spanish speakers, and more, which you can access by visiting **RealFaith.com** or downloading the **RealFaith app**.

With a master's degree in exegetical theology from Western Seminary in Portland, Oregon, he has spent the better part of his life teaching verse-by-verse through books of the Bible, contextualizing its timeless truths and never shying away from challenging, convicting passages that speak to the heart of current cultural dilemmas.

Together, Mark and Grace have co-authored "Win your War", "Real Marriage", and "Real Romance: Sex in the Song of Songs", and he co-authored a father-daughter project called "Pray Like Jesus" with his daughter, Ashley. Pastor Mark has also written numerous other books including "Spirit-Filled Jesus", "Who Do You Think You Are?", "Vintage Jesus", and "Doctrine".

If you have any prayer requests for us, questions for future Ask Pastor Mark or Dear Grace videos, or a testimony regarding how God has used this and other resources to help you learn God's Word, we would love to hear from you at **hello@realfaith.com**.